PATRICIO ROZAS

EXPERIENCES AND RECOMMENDATIONS OF AN ENTREPRENEUR

Act with courage and never give up

Copyright 2019

All the rights reserved
Published by Patricio Rozas
Amazon Kindle Direct Publishing.

41.378 words

First Edition
December 2019
ISBN 9781651946510

PATRICIO ROZAS

EXPERIENCES AND RECOMMENDATIONS OF AN ENTREPRENEUR

Act with courage and **NEVER GIVE UP**

I dedicate this, my first book, to my three children, Paula, Patricio and Benjamín and to my grandson Vicente, another child that came into our lives.

I have written this book for them, with all my love, affection and respect as they have always been very brave throughout their lives. They have taught me with their example to live and face life with immense courage.

They are wonderful people and I love them with all my heart.

INDEX

With thanks to 11

Words of the Author 14

Introduction 15

Get started 21

    My childhood 22
        The dreams of a boy 27
    My adolescence 28
        An injury left me a lot of interesting lessons 31

Learn 37

    Making important decisions in my life. 40
    The stage of mentors and guides starts 43
    The importance of effort 45
    The importance of achievements 47

Work 48

    The beginnings of my working life 49
    The Need to Belong 51
    Be careful of scarcity and decline 55

Choose and start your own business 57

    Growth in the job I liked 58
    Becoming Independent 62
    The early times of Independence 63
    Beginnings of Leadership and my first
        fall 65
    Planning Exercise 67

Don't be afraid of falling 78

    The origin of a dramatic fall 79

Breaking up a marriage 81
The loss of two beloved people 83
   Supporting my children to help them overcome hard times 85

Significant Economic Loss 87

Never give up 91

Starting to make the company steady . 94
Challenges once the company is steady
.... 98
A new challenge 101

Grow 110

Expanding and diversifying in the
   mining industry 111
A different way to see life 113

Make Contributions 114

My experience with Tony Robbins 115
   The Need of Certainty. 119
   The Need of Variety 119
   The Need to feel important. 120
   The Need to feel connected. 121
   The Need to grow 121
   The Need to make contributions or Give 122

Suggestions for entrepreneurs 124

   Having a dream is the first requirement 127
   Finding the time is the first step 129
   Attitude -Certainty 132
   The beginning of the day 136
   Commitment 138
   Trust 140
   Beliefs 141
   Determination 142
   Discipline 144
   Leadership 148
   Optimism 149

Passion 154
Positive Thinking..158
Posture 159
Resilience 160
Vision 162

Clients 165
Empathy..166
Heart 168
Trust 169
Value 170

Collaborators... 172
Communications..173
Empowerment 175
Active Listening 177
Get people involved..178

Growth 179
Economic and financial issues........................180
Export 182
Assets 184
Indirect Growth..185

Challenges... 186
Attitude 187
Learn 191
Anticipate..192
Look for a way out..194
Focus on solutions 195
How to achieve dreams?..................................197
Details 199
Experience 201
Constant Improvement 202
Opportunities..203

Strategy 204
Strategy...205
Anchors – Important......................................209
Change of Paradigm..210
Perseverance and Trust....................................211
Make Contributions 213
Limiting Beliefs 214
Diversification...216
Flexibility and Planning 220

Innovation 221
Achievements 223
Measure 224
Look upwards...231
Momentum 233
Negotiation 234
Complex Situations..236
Get out of a business..238
Value 241
Variety 244
Vision 245

Skills 246
Constant Improvement..249

Marketing 251
Creation of a brand..252
Personality...254
Real time..256
Innovation...257
Without pressure...259

One more dream.. 260
Educate..261

Patricio Rozas.. 266

Studies 267
Business Skills. 267
Specialization Courses 268

With thanks to

I have dreamt of writing a book for a long time. This one is a small tribute to my children, Paula, Patricio and Benjamín, to their mother Paula who had accompanied me for many years, and to the people who have helped me in this process of growing as a person and entrepreneur.

I would like to thank especially my mother. She is the first person I want and must be grateful to for being able to write this book. Without her, I would simply not be part of this world, nor would my children exist. She had always been, without knowing up to which extent, the first and most powerful engine of my life and my best teacher. Without her, without her humble but indestructible honesty and infinite and unconditional love, I would have never become the man I am today.

My children have always been the main drivers in this journey to entrepreneurship. They have always supported me to go on growing both as a businessman and as a person.

My eldest daughter Paula did not have me at her side for many years because I had to work thousands of kilometers away from home. I generally visited her once a month, for the shifts we had consisted in 22 working days with 8 days to rest and, to this we had to add the days commuting took us for many years.

A beautiful day, Patricio was born. Having already two children, I thought it was not possible to go on working far from home and that I had sufficient reasons to do what was necessary to be with them and to see them grow and experience the happiness of being close to them. When Patricio turned one, I started to think I had to do something different, for I could not continue with the same work load I had had so far. I gave it a lot of thought, until I finally decided to go back home and set on a new journey. The decision had already been made. I would start to set up a business similar to the one I had always worked for to provide for my family.

Sometime later, my son Benjamín was born and he has accompanied me through every moment up to the present time when I am writing this book.

I also want to thank all those who believed in me and opened every door I knocked on in my journey to become an entrepreneur; and also all those who were at my side in the good and bad times and who have always lent me their ears, their hands and shoulders in case of need.

As a businessman I have devoted my whole life to the metal mechanical field. For this reason, I want to express my gratitude to the companies that have trusted me and gave me the opportunity to assist them with projects, solutions, strategies

WITH THANKS TO

and documents. It has been an honor to be the provider of such important companies.

I am deeply grateful to all those who have cooperated in the growth of the companies I represent. I want to express special gratitude to all the people who have accompanied me for so long in my activities and profession, in good and bad times, in very bad and excellent times. Thanks to their immense support I have acquired significant knowledge.

And I finally acknowledge my gratitude to the hundreds of books I have read in my life, and which have impacted on my personal growth with their motivation and enthusiasm, enabling me to access a higher level of thought.

Each day we can take a small or big step towards our dreams, without any restriction at all. All we need is to think and to believe with all our heart that we can achieve something. If you do it in this way, without any doubt, you will achieve it.

Words of the Author

Many people who know me closely and some others who only know me from the industry, often ask me how to get started and recover from falls in life. I always answer with my truth that is very simple: My answer is that If I fill myself with positive thinking, at every step of my journey, an inner voice will appear and lead me to answer a single question: "how can I meet my objective?" This question silences the other inner voice, the one of fear, which tells me not to try anymore and wants to convince me there are no reasons to go on.

When we decide to challenge ourselves with the conviction that we can achieve it, there is no obstacle that might stop us.

There will be falls, but we have to stand back on our feet. The best option for me has always been to have a positive attitude in every situation, no matter how difficult it might seem.

Nobody wants to fail in life, but we have to understand that success does not only refer to economic success. There is a deeper satisfaction originated in growing and reaching our dreams, which creates an inner power full of energy.

This power will encourage you to move ahead. And the day will come when you will manage to get the reward for all the sacrifice and effort devoted to your business.

Act with courage and NEVER GIVE UP

Introduction

After many years, I have determined that it is necessary and fundamental for me to write a book in which I can clearly explain my experiences and recommendations as a businessman.

I feel I empathize very well with ordinary people, because I am an ordinary man and so I want to share my personal history, my life and my experience today with those who already are or would like to be businessmen. I want to give an account of what my life was like and what it meant to me, how I spent my childhood, my adolescence, and how I evolved as time went by to become a businessman.

I anticipate to all those who will read this book that it was mainly written to help them fulfill their dreams and encourage their beliefs. We should all rethink our lives, no matter what might happen.

And what is more important: we should always have a dream, and the only thing we need to make it come true is just doing and doing, but doing with passion and optimism. You should think how to get started and go on growing, and you must promise not to get to a standstill at any time.

The most important lesson I have learnt during all these years and due to all I have gone through is that to make a dream come true you must feel empathy. Empathy is achieved when we understand people, clients, partners, consumers, employees, suppliers, the competence and the community. It is important to see what the others know, feel and need.

It was fundamental to identify at every moment what they knew, what they felt and what they needed.

It is important to develop empathy once you have decided to start your own business. It is impossible to move forward without knowing those around you.

I have gone through difficult situations in my life and I have always felt the need to stand back on my feet when hope was about to vanish into thin air. And I learnt that challenges in life are opportunities to grow and improve.

The objective of this book is to help those who need to conquer these challenges. On many occasions, we can handle them but, instead of facing them, we are paralyzed. We know that we have to talk to our employees in the field, but many times we prefer to stay comfortable in our offices ignoring what the others may feel.

In this book, I managed to put in order and introduce all the subjects I have dealt with in my life and which forced me to undergo deep change as I moved on, both in the personal and

INTRODUCTION

professional realms. They are closely related and one affects the other either positively or negatively, whether you want it or not.

It is fundamental to be convinced that if you fall, you can get back on your feet. You must be aware that you have to go for a walk every day, to knock on doors, make calls and remember names and, to be always convinced that you can achieve anything; we cannot accept an unfavorable scenario in our minds.

You have to take care of your business but you also have to take care of you. You have to look after your health, not only after your body but after your thoughts and emotions, because you also need to have all the strength, will and certainty that will drive you to fulfill your dreams.

I call this, healthy thoughts, emotions and attitude. Attitude means, according to the dictionary, keeping the right posture in the face of circumstances. I can´t see myself defeated and round-shouldered in life. I must stand in an upright position and be convinced I will manage to do it, and that if I do not achieve something, I will insist. Perseverance means healthy thoughts and is the key to the success of any entrepreneur.

You should always think how to build a change in you to get started and then grow and keep on growing. And we need to count with a plan to maintain this change and growth. Life puts us in front of many drawbacks, and we must overcome them to prove ourselves we can do it.

Can we build something with a small amount of money? Yes, this is the reason of this book. I started with very little money; I grew, fell, got back on my feet, then grew again, fell again and got back on my feet again. And in every case, I learnt and improved. That is the reason why I am convinced I can help many people.

This is not a book of personal finance, it is a book of growth, of development and business and personal self-help.

I will help you to look ahead when you experience drawbacks. I want my words to help you struggle against any obstacle you might encounter in life. It is about acting with courage, always certain you will make it. Because if you believe you will, it will certainly happen. If you are convinced, your body and your mind will get aligned to achieve it.

I want this book to contain plenty of ideas so that everyone, with skills and intelligence, can grow; and if there are falls, to ease their pain. I want you to find tools in my words. I think life is built with experiences, examples, dreams, passion and perseverance.

For this reason I want you to concentrate on the mission of your life and to direct your eyes towards what you have dreamt of; and if you fall, I want you to get back on your feet and run forwards. If you happen to stumble again, this book will help you to get back on your feet and keep on running until you reach your dreams, your desires and the life you want to live.

I have always thought people who can carry out important things have to take action and do them. For this reason, I have shared my life here, since my childhood to the date this is being published, giving details of how it has evolved in time.

Those who want to make changes in their lives, have everything to do it. I intend this book to be your inspiration, because it contains real experiences, in which every obstacle I had to overcome represented the opportunity to learn.

I wish you could open your mind and think with obsession until you reach your highest desires in life. I did not use the term obsession by chance, but because we have to concentrate, we cannot let our present or past thoughts stop and paralyze us.

My idea of this book is to transform it into a practical guide to allow you to rethink your life and, if you feel identified with my words, at any moment you cannot move forward, use it as a manual TO MAKE PROGRESS IN LIFE.

For the sake of this progress, I decided to base my book on the verbs to which we should pay attention. These are:

- Get started
- Learn
- Work

- Find
- Start a business
- Don´t be afraid of falling
- Never give up
- Grow
- Make contributions

What have I learnt?

I have learnt that in the life of an entrepreneur ALL these stages appear on a daily basis.

Every day, we start something, we learn something, we work, start a business and we also fall. Never give up and even more important, grow and make contributions.

Thanks for letting me cooperate with you.

Patricio Rozas

Get started

*We always have different paths to take.
If you are thinking you can reorganize your
live, do not forget you have full control of your life
through your thoughts.*

My childhood

I am the youngest of seven siblings, all more than ten years senior than me. My father passed away when I was 4 days old and we were extremely poor; we did not even have a television.

I lived in a house that belonged to the railway company. My father worked for that railway company and our house was built with rail dormants. Dormants are the supporting bases on which rails are built for the circulation of trains. Our house was of the same material, which in fact was highly resistant and still exists today. More than 60 years went by, and it could even resist many earthquakes that occurred here in Chile.

In the next page I´ll share with you a picture taken this year 2019 of a visit to the house of my childhood. I went there on a Monday to remember my origins, a few days before this book was published. The house has now been turned into a railway warehouse.

Every day, I thank having had my mother, Julia Rosa Gallardo Salinas, because she taught me values. She always smiled to me, and this smile made me understand how much she trusted me. I know this was my blessing, because many people never have the pure love of a mother. The love of a mother represents huge immaterial wealth.

In spite of all the deprivations I had to go through when I was a child, I had to choose between two paths, the path to grow or the path to follow the wrong steps of the others. **This was the biggest lesson I learnt as a child, to be able to take good decisions.**

I have always chosen the first path. As a child, it was to grow up by my mother´s side, and to help her with her chores. I helped her after school and at weekends, and my duties consisted in helping her with the agricultural activities in a land where we worked on results.

I always wanted to do more, so since I was a child I tried to find a way to make a living, for example, washing my neighbors´ cars. I volunteered and the neighbors paid me what their conscious dictated was fair.

As a child, it was very important for me to have some money at the end of the day and give it to my mother, who needed it to be able to maintain our home and bring food to our table. As I grew up, I learnt what it meant to be responsible and contributed to the house I lived in.

As time went by, I understood that this "house" started to get bigger. After some time, it included my own family and thousands of families in my life as a businessman. I could not always do this successfully, as there were times when I fell dramatically and this taught me important lessons.

When I was a little child, around seven, I also went to the market to sell vegetables. I used to tell myself that if I looked for it, I would always find a chance to help more.

I remember that near my house there was a company that accumulated straw in our land. Mixed with the straw there were heads of garlic that I picked up and sold at the corner of this same market I used to go to.

The second path I could have taken was following the decisions of some other people in the neighborhood but I chose not to. At that time, we were children and we played football or marbles together on the streets. There were some children, older than us, who unfortunately, even when sharing the same friends, came and treated us badly or punched us.

I could have joined them and engaged in their misbehavior. If I had chosen that option, I would have been part of this group and made sure that they would not mistreat us anymore, and I would have certainly followed their steps.

Always get together with healthy people. Who you choose to be with, talks about yourself.

I have always had a strong personality and have always been convinced that I had the obligation to help my mother. I remember having asked God to grant me the possibility of keeping my mother alive till I could make my own living. I prayed every night so that I could start working as soon as possible to help her so that she didn´t have to work so hard.

On one occasion, as we were working the land, my mother fainted. I remember the immense anguish I experienced and I desperately burst into tears. When I saw her lying on the ground, motionless, I felt my mother was going to die, and I found myself each day invaded by the anguish of thinking that without my mother, I would have nobody to share my life with.

My older brothers and sisters were somewhere else and living other lives. They worried about their lives and unfortunately, not all of them, but three of my brothers had drinking problems. My other brother was deeply involved in his activities and had been absent for a long time doing the military service. Of my two sisters, one was married and the other, even if she was living with us, was focused on her life and her friends.

The dreams of a boy

As a boy, I dreamt of being a singer and, within my possibilities, I used to practice. I loved singing as my favorite singers did. I started to practice a lot and I also developed an interest in sports, among them, baseball, rhythmic gymnastics, football and others.

My real sportive life was a 100% focused on football. I trained a lot and, regarded it as an interesting way to grow. People used to tell me to insist and train a lot, as they saw big chances of my becoming a professional football player.

My adolescence

Once again, as in my childhood, I had to take decisions in life.

I liked sports, so I started to play since I was a little boy, and when I was 13, I was already playing for the honor divisions of amateur football. I decided to devote my entire efforts, and in the same year I started, I was promoted to the first division of amateur football.

It was an important period of my life, because rarely were 13-year-old boys given the opportunity to play in adult teams, or the privilege of doing it in the first division of amateur football. That was a time when I really felt highly valued.

I went to tournaments where football players playing for highly recognized clubs participated. I was very proud when I was offered to be tried at professional clubs of the inferior divisions; I had the chance to be incorporated to the permanent team in two clubs near my neighborhood.

As I was making progress in the clubs, I was also making progress in my studies. However, it was very complicated to organize myself every day, as I also had to work during my free time to earn some money and help my mother with the household. I had to do something to earn money and, so I started to work part time in a factory that was being set up at the same place where I did some repairs of chicken feeding trays. As it was already written in my life destiny, I was forced to learn two tasks: mechanics and welding. Who could have guessed at that time that they would determine my destiny forever?

It was obvious that the welding tasks we carried out were not very important, they were mainly small and very specific tasks, but they provided me with the money I needed to take home. I gave my mother everything I earned and I always remember that when I wanted to give it all to her, she used to tell me: "Son, you always need to carry some money in your pockets and you need to be dressed smartly. And you know why, son? Because people will judge you by your looks". My mother had always been very wise when it came to giving advice.

Being around 14 years old, I once told my mother: "I will never stop helping you, mother; I don´t want you to work anymore. I will help you for the rest of my life. I want you to live many years more, and I need you to accompany me on my journey. I will demonstrate you that I will be an important person in life". This statement turned into a promise I deeply kept in my heart and which I still keep even after she left me.

As time went by, I was transferred to the third division of professional football, where at the age of 16, I disputed the reserve slot with another goal keeper. Finally I obtained the reserve slot for a well known professional player.

I was so into being a starter that in training games I always played at least one entire half of the game. I did my best to become a starter in the team.

GET STARTED

An injury left me a lot of interesting lessons.

I was once playing a game in the third division of a club that was struggling to be promoted to the professional category. They had three goal keepers and a fourth one, so that they could constantly evaluate their evolution and always have three in the team.

I started as fourth goal keeper, and then I moved on to be the third one. I started to be tested and I became the second, so I started playing in the second half after the starter. In short, I replaced the substitute player.

When I was playing a game against a professional team, I had a kick off in the goal box. It was a strong kick to the net originated in the middle of the pitch, and as it was so strong and I was trying to cover the net, the ball produced a rebound. The ball was then in the perfect position to be passed to a player at the corner. He kicked the ball with all his strength, I was positioned at the same place and I jumped again, I remember, to my left. It wasn´t a flying save as goal keepers call it, I was trying to stop the ball when it hit me very strongly on my left finger.

Life itself is like this, you can stop a challenge, but if you do not take control of it and produce a rebound, it will come again for a second time and will turn into a problem.

This act resulted in an injury, which was not well treated at the time, and prevented me from playing for more than three months. The only thing I received from the club was a phone call, nothing else. The life of players is like this, and so is the life of workers.

Obviously, I had to manage on my own and it was there when I started thinking if I really wanted to continue with sports. The intention was latent, but the truth is that I had to give priority to what would generate income.

It was precisely as far as income was concerned, that I felt the club did not support me and, I was partly disappointed to see that dreams could be spoilt so easily, as I received no help from the club. In fact, I felt they had forgotten me.

I expected that due to the injury, the club´s managers would be worried about my health. I still had the hope of their asking or helping me with the basic medical expenses I had to incur in. Unfortunately, I was terribly sad to see this never happened.

I had to conceal my physical and emotional suffering and I had to work with a lot of pain, both physical and emotional. In spite of the fact that my mother kept on working, I never stopped helping her with the household.

The club was not interested in supporting talented people; they only supported the healthiest and strongest ones. Over time, I learnt that it is very difficult for a businessman to take care of all the talented people, because they had to be supported in many areas of life and not only in their jobs.

I was highly disappointed by football; I did not want to keep on remembering what had occurred. At this age, I had to make a decision again.

These were moments of decision making, for I had to choose between working or studying. I would have loved to study, I was talented, but I couldn´t go on studying at the university due to the high costs. I did not have the means to do it, my studies required to devote the whole day to the university, and this would consume all the time I also needed to go on working and helping my mother at home.

At the age of 16, my destiny showed me the only and true path I had in front of me, and this was working. It was an important decision as I had to look for a job before turning 17, which would take place in March of the following year.

Over the years, I also understood that the decision had not been between "studying" or "working" as many young people and adults tend to think. Today, wiser as a consequence of aging,

I can see that this decision was between "university studies" or "field studies". I did not go to the university, but I never stopped studying and learning. I just did it on a daily basis, being supported by mentors, courses and life itself. I did not study methodically. I also had to learn to establish priorities. We always have paths to choose and, I always chose to move forward, look into the future and grow, and this attitude is in my opinion, the base of sound development and growth.

Having clear and accurate objectives allows you to move forward not paying attention to obstacles, we only have to focus on the objective we have right now and never neglect what we are doing, whatever it might take.

We have to be the children of rigor, even if it takes a lot of effort and sacrifice.

You have to keep on moving forward in life. Nothing can stop the dreams of what you want to do. We have to remember that we can all achieve several goals, if we simply think we can.

The objective is to keep your attention in the priority you have right now. And to start dreaming and working in your dreams every day, clearly convinced you can always move on in your dreams. The main idea is to have big dreams and transform them into your obsession.

Do not forget that life enables you to get where your thoughts can get to and expand. Bear in mind that your dreams are part of your same thoughts; that they are inter-related in accordance with your obsession and, if your obsession is very intense you have to incorporate it to your daily life. It is like this that you will manage to make your dreams come true.

The progress you make will be they way in which you will constantly give shape to all the things that you have always focused on, to all these dreams that are part of your obsessions and impulses. This is also achieved with a positive attitude and the desire to fulfill your dreams. Remember that on many occasions certain things are likely to happen and will discourage you from going on, it is then when you have to think that anything that happens is part of the growth you wish to achieve.

Some people become motionless when problems and situations occur in their lives, but do not forget that if you keep on going, the day will come when you finally reach your dreams and wishes. This is certainly something magic that takes place when your attention remains in what you want so dearly and always remember that when we want to do something we have to do it right away not on the next day.

Be determined to do it immediately, not the following week or month or year, do it right now. Often, many things might happen in the meantime. Frequently, we missed the opportunity due to the time we waste. Make the decision and do it without hesitating. Remember that dreams are always built with sacrifice and effort. You should be focused on the results that will gradually appear provided you do your best to make your dreams come true. Maintain your obsessive thinking and dreams and the desire to be a different person in life.

You have to focus your conscious self obsessively on what you want to achieve, only thinking that you can achieve it and with no fear of getting further. Never forget you need a strong obsession for great dreams, those we think are impossible to fulfill. We can mention many cases of people who have made great dreams come true because they believed in their dreams and desires. However, this book does not intend this; it intends to make you believe in yourself and in your dreams, to help you stand back on your feet after failure and keep your conscious mind focused on achieving the life you would like to live.

Think when you want to achieve your dreams. Perhaps in five years? So, you will have to work bearing this time in mind. Your dreams might be projected in a more distant future, so you will need some elements and people capable of helping you to achieve it sooner. Remember that the more ambitious our dreams are, the more obstacles and difficulties we will face. Nevertheless, I beg you to print yourself with positive thinking, for this thinking will help you overcome all the drawbacks you may face in life.

Learn

The Origin of Experience.
When you desire to go on learning, you will finally become engaged.

LEARN 39

In the previous page I included a photo of my studies with John Grinder, one of the creators of the Neurolinguistic Programming (NLP).

Making important decisions in my life.

At the age of 16, I understood I couldn´t go on studying, so I started to look for a job. I focused on working alternatives that offered the payment of my social security, health insurance and all the benefits covered by a working contract. So far, all the jobs I had had consisted in minor tasks due to the time I needed to study.

I started as a worker at the construction site that was being carried out for an important company for which I used to repair chicken feed trays in my neighborhood. I started working with the construction spade, the brick hammer and the wheelbarrow. It was at that time when I started building my personality and when my inner strength grew.

During the construction works, I started paying attention to the people that came to the company to perform the installation of big structures and equipment. It was then when I developed a deep interest in making conversation

LEARN

with the specialists that got there to carry out these tasks. I noticed that they brought their own people and that I had no chance of working with them.

I kept on asking myself why I had no chances. I could not see why, if I had and showed my desire to do so, I couldn´t be in this group of specialists. It was a revelation, because I created inside myself the habit of speculating: how could I make the things I wanted to happen in fact happen? I soon understood that the key question was "**How?**" I had to look for alternatives and I had to find who to talk to about this subject.

When we say "I can´t" or "I don´t know", we get paralyzed.
What we have to ask ourselves is "how can I do it?"
It is there that your body, mind and soul start to act together.

I started to think and finally understood that the first step was to look for someone who helped me find the answers.

I knew I didn´t have to look for the answers in people who did not have them, as me, and I finally found the answer: "we have to ask the person who knows the most and who is within our reach". I had to talk to the engineer in charge of the whole construction site. I waited for the appropriate occasion and I approached him to get his suggestions and advice. He observed me with calm after I had introduced myself and expressed my desire to work with the specialists and answered to me: "Look kid, you have to talk to the chief of the construction site; he is the one who knows if he can give you any task as **helper**". It was perfect, for even at this early age, I knew that helping was the seed of experience.

The stage of mentors and guides starts

When the engineer told me that I had to talk to the chief of the construction site to offer myself as a prospective helper, I was happy. I wanted to be an assistant, because I considered this was the way to learn the ropes from scratch. It is different to learn them at a classroom in theory; it means moving and doing from the very beginning observing reality. I was very interested in seeing masters carrying out their tasks

> *Over the years, I learnt that being a helper of a person who has a vast knowledge is called "Shadow Mentoring".*
> *Being the helper of a person who knows the most of a subject is the most effective way of learning an activity.*

Like this, I managed to draw the attention of the chiefs who noticed the interest I had and gave me the opportunity to be the helper of a welder. I was deeply moved and I still feel moved when I remember these days, when I learnt that getting two elements together could be a powerful metaphor in business.

I remember my attitude; I got very early in the morning to prepare all the materials and machines for the welder so that he could arrive and start welding right away. As time went by, I incorporated new welding terminology: fillet, fix, upwards and horizontal positions, flat, over heads, pipe welding, tin, lead, antimony and lead welding, and tens of new terms, hundreds, inches, numbers, centimeters, millimeters, lights and so many others that made a completely new and fascinating world enter my life. I enjoyed every single minute. I had always had the passion to study, to feel the sparks, the energy, to wear protective gear and eye protective gear. My heart beat fast every time I learnt new details.

Eventually, the master could see the real interest I had due to my devoted involvement; I was always ready to **anticipate** to his needs and the situations that might generate so that he had everything he required. The most important thing for me was that he could work efficiently.

Time went by, and one day I was ready and brave enough to ask him for an opportunity to let me practice during lunch time. He said he couldn´t because at that time he wanted me to have lunch. I quickly answered that I could spend less time having lunch to be able to start practicing. I needed to learn and to demonstrate that I really liked the job. He was a great teacher, because he gave me the responsibility, saying that if I was really interested and really wanted it, then it all depended on me.

He was clear enough to tell me that if he saw I did not demonstrate any interest to learn or if he saw a lack of enthusiasm on my part, he would definitely stop supporting me.

This meant no benefit for him, on the contrary. They didn´t accept at that time because the union was very selfish and thought that by giving me an opportunity they would have had a very young competitor.

The importance of effort

My constant perseverance led me to ask for permission to stay longer in the afternoons to go on working. As I was gaining their confidence, they little by little accepted my offer and let me stay till later. This confidence was built not only as a result of my attitude but of my increasing aptitude for the job. They could see that I had made significant progress, and after three months I was given the possibility of obtaining a welding qualification.

I gathered all my interest and desire and managed to be, at the age of 17, a welder specialized in pipes. It was and still is a huge achievement to have been able to obtain at such an early age the maximum specialization of the industrial assembly in the field of metal mechanics. I am very proud to point out that such a merit was out of proportions at that time.

With sheer determination, self confidence and maturity, I started to practice my job as a certified worker.

Although later on, this construction site where I had learnt was over and I didn´t see the people I had met there any more, all these experiences left a mark in me. Undoubtedly, that time represented for me a period of immense growth.

The importance of achievements

When this construction was over, I changed to a new one. But, due to my young age, it was not surprising they didn´t want to give me the responsibility I had gained in the previous construction site as a pipe welding specialist. So, I had to start all over again and work as an assistant welder.

One day, when the main welder did not turn up to work, and there was an urgent task to be done, I reminded them that I was qualified and knew how to do the job. They told me to demonstrate it, and I did so, without hesitation, as I perfectly knew what I was doing. My achievements made them aware of my aptitudes, and this together with my attitude, immediately resulted in my appointment as main welder. The following day, to everybody´s surprise, I was welding.

What was fundamental in this stage is that thanks to my achievements I never stopped growing in the specialization.

Work

The Origin of Commitment.

Not only do you have to be a businessman, your workers have to consider you a leader in the field.

The beginnings of my working life

Growing as a worker, requires a lot of effort, engagement and the permanent search of new alternatives that will enable us to build a career in a job where there are increasingly more and more specialties and aptitudes. The specializations and aptitudes we cultivate represent our main value.

I started with renewed energy and clearly convinced that there were more possibilities in the different industries and that I had to make the effort and sacrifice to learn all I could about every single subject related to the industries I was interested in.

So far, I had learnt a lot about welding and I knew I had to learn about the industry. I also realized that I had to understand people more; there were profound histories in the lives of the people carrying out these tasks. In general, specialists took great care of their job and did not provide information to anybody. Sometimes, the reason was their greed, some others their fear. This fear was explained by the idea that if more people learnt their jobs, their high salaries would be reduced. This would make an impact on their income and the comfortable life they led thanks to the high salaries these important companies paid them.

It was then that I started to have the dream I am materializing now, of having an International Academy of Specialized Welding to provide continuous work to those who want to specialize in this fascinating world I am part of.

The Need to Belong

Who has never felt the need to belong to a group? I have. I have always been eager to learn and be part of something and, in fact, I managed to, as I could start working in the field I had trained for. I always knew that I had to learn from my seniors and I could see that belonging to this group was the way to approach highly specialized people. I wanted to make friends with them and the way to do it was sharing social activities after work.

Many specialists at that time, used to drink a lot of alcohol, because there was an old belief that said that as welders, they had to drink wine to prevent the smoke originated in welding from getting into their lungs. Was it just a limiting belief or was it an excuse to indulge in the pleasures of life without any restriction?

If the smoke issue was true then, I couldn´t understand why they smoked like chimneys, even when they were constantly inhaling the smoke from welding and on top of that they made it even worse by drinking wine, "supposedly to clean their lungs". I was really surprised, for I knew how wrong this way of living was and, I was even more surprised to see how all this put safety at work at risk. I was convinced that leading this life, the likelihood of injuries increased and I remembered what I had felt when I got injured while playing football as a young boy.

Would by any chance companies worry about these specialists if they got injured or fell ill due to this life style?

At that time I decided to get closer to them getting to know their habits and talking in detail about how they performed their welding tasks. Like this, I learnt more and more, at tables abundant in smoke and booze, I got all the information I needed to gather. But at the same time, I tried to blend in so that they considered me an important part of the team and they could see my interest in becoming part of them. I only wanted to learn from their immense know-how and experience.

I was convinced that they had to teach me because I was their mate at leisure times and shared their vices. In the afternoons we gathered to drink wine and we smoked without stopping. I shared the same ideas and I enjoyed the anecdotes they told of their long years of working as welders. I used to praise their feats, all of them anecdotes of the construction of important industries, where these specialists contributed with their know-how.

I had to organize in my mind all the information I gathered when they were already drunk as it was then when they gave the most important details to be taken into consideration. Like this, I could clear my doubts, storing in my mind the secrets of their task. I distinguished the most capable and outstanding ones, because when I applied their lessons I managed to obtain the result I expected.

Be careful of scarcity and decline

Living with a lack of love and the decay produced by life pleasures also made feel all the adventures they went through while they were away from home. Their children had been born, but as they were not at home with their family, their only concern was to send them money. Sometimes, they spent months without knowing the son that had been born. For me, it was difficult to follow this nostalgic spirit of living far from home, unable to see my children grow.

All the specialists went on working, but an important part of them missed work due to their excessive drinking habits. At the same time, as working people with some money in their pockets, they got involved with prostitutes. This resulted in many of them abandoning their homes for other women, many times out of love, many others out of lust.

It is not necessary to be a fortune teller to know that most of the times, these people ended up on the streets, broken and losing their families and their prestige at work. Their limiting beliefs and egos were so big that they couldn´t realize how vice could take over them and destroy their lives.

This showed me an extremely cruel reality and I learnt what we shouldn´t do in life. Then I went back to the growing path. I focused my growth on specializing in everything related to the welding world.

I always recommend getting away from the wrong path; it is possible if we really want to. Indulging in bad habits is just an excuse to take the easy path, to avoid hard work. We should concentrate on learning and growing following the right path, always.

Choose and start your own business

The Origin of dreams

Growth in the job I liked

Dreams originate in the activities we enjoy.

After having worked and shared lots of experiences with specialists, and as time went by, I started to visit different parts of the country. I learnt from their industries and I learnt to implement all the knowledge I was acquiring about diversification in this job. This stage was really enriching as I worked for different companies, with different materials and complex welding procedures. I went through this stage with strict and hard work and during this inner process I grew in every possible way. I was then ready to perform different certifications for welding procedures and I had access to the state of the art methods and tasks existing at that moment.

My perseverance allowed me to get to important places and I must be thankful for having a natural empathy to deal with people and this has enabled me to find really valuable people on my journey.

But, as I was growing, a lot of envy generated around me, for I started to have more options, more benefits, and was more qualified in the job than many who had a longer experience than mine.

At 22, I was offered to work as a supplier. I did not want to be a contractor unless I had a fix position and the safety required to set on this journey.

I remained like this for more than 6 years, carrying out rather specialized tasks. I also worked on resting days. I was always told that due to my knowledge and mindset, I could perfectly well set up my own company. At the beginning, this wasn´t the best option for me, because I wanted to go on learning growing in my field.

Working with the highest standards of international companies and getting to know the most important projects in Chile was my own university.

From the age of 21 to 29 I worked in different parts of the country and thus experienced what it was like to work and collect high salaries, or in locations far away from cities, almost limiting with other countries, separated by mountain ranges and deserts.

The origin of dreams acquires real strength when we start to generate savings.

After having worked for so long in adverse conditions, I started to elaborate on the idea of setting up my own company.

I strongly concentrated on saving and making investments. I had bought two very big plots of land, and after having also acquired all the necessary equipment to start operating, I only had USD 100,000 left to start my company. I also managed to buy two trucks and all the necessary tools for two permanent teams of people to work in my start up.

CHOOSE AND START YOU OWN BUSINESS

When I felt ready, I started to have meetings, as is commonly said, to knock on different doors. Then I learnt a very important lesson I always transmit to my coworkers: the appropriate documents have to be ready before starting any activity. I followed every step required to start my activities and for the legal and financial organization of my company. I did it little by little until I had all the required papers. I knew my time had come.

Starting my life as an entrepreneur was no easy decision. I had thought it over for quite a long time and the idea started to appear in my mind and finally I took the decision. And this is how I set on the journey I still follow today.

Becoming Independent

I had already decided to start and I had all the paperwork approved. The next step was to have the invoice checkbooks made and to go to the bank to be assigned a current account to do payments. I was fed up of living on the mountains and deserts far away from cities and from home.

The decision had already been taken. I rejected an important contract, losing some bonuses I had been offered and the value of which was quite significant at that time. I was certain that if I didn't make that decision then, I would never start my own business.

So, with the savings from the jobs I had done for those international companies plus the invested equipment, I had the chance to hire over 20 people. I had two very big plots of land. However, I lived in a 72 square meter flat. I clearly knew I couldn't waste my money and build an expensive house. The first thing I had to do was to make the base of my dreams stronger, and later start thinking about comfort.

The final step was to be given the current account, which I finally got with a small credit line of USD 1,000. I knew it wouldn't be easy, but I was determined and convinced that even if it was difficult I had to go through that experience.

I imagined that learning about the financial world was similar to the learning process I had already lived when I had started working and that had been completely successful. So, on January 13th, 1998 I quit my job as an employee and I started the journey of a freelance worker.

The early times of Independence

I had always thought that my first experience as a free lance entrepreneur would have been with the company with which I had worked the most in the last years.

But unfortunately, the company that had always asked me to be a contractor did not give me the chance when I thought it would support me automatically hiring the services of the company I had created.

It was then that I discovered that the first important challenge an entrepreneur faces from the very start is to create its client portfolio.

A few people would trust a company that is starting from scratch, or as I learnt are called "startups". I realized that the entire picture I had created in my mind was wrong.

I needed to encourage a highly positive way of thinking in my mind to make up for the huge disappointment I had suffered when the company that had mostly encouraged my independence had literally said NO.

I also learnt from experience that we should not take a NO for an answer and, that we have to be positive and look for other alternatives to obtain a YES.

Finally I found some smaller companies where I started to practice my profession and where I was received and assigned tasks generally at weekends.

Beginnings of Leadership and my first fall

In this way, I managed to start gathering my team. At first it consisted in 10 workers and then I could increase it to the 20 people I had originally planned to have. The onset was highly complex, but fortunately I had a lot of experience and training in estimates and in the management of personnel thanks to the international companies I had worked for.

During the first 3 years, what I was earning was not enough to pay for salaries and cover fix costs. It was like this that I experienced my first serious failure: I lost 100,000 dollars, I had to sell the land that was worth 70,000 dollars and I lost everything, everything at all. Three years working with my heart and soul doing minor jobs, to end up broken.

Life had taught me that I had to pay the price of starting without knowing all I needed about the complex business world. It was really complex, but not difficult. It wasn´t really that difficult, but required a wide variety of information, administrative and labor information that could be responsible for making me lose any margin in an operation if slightly mismanaged. It was then, when the first dreams of transmitting these experiences to those who wanted to become entrepreneurs were born.

I had learnt something fundamental for a novice entrepreneur as me, and it was that the key factor of success is to reserve a percentage of sales as a fund to overcome unexpected results. I was starting a journey in my life when I would learn that the main challenge was to take control of unforeseen situations on a daily basis.

Being a businessman means to learn to foresee different administrative, human, strategic and financial scenarios that might appear permanently and continuously.

It is not the same to collect late than early, it is not the same to fall behind in the first half of the period of a project than in the second half.

Let me share an exercise I have learnt some years afterwards and which would have helped me if been applied to a problem I encountered at that time.

Planning Exercise

Imagine a project divided into 4 time units. These can consist in days, weeks, months or years. And imagine that after finishing the first of the 4 time units, we are informed that there will be a deviation of another time unit, changing the original planning to five units. That´s to say, at least an additional month of salary pay, costs and management. The graph on a board would be as follows:

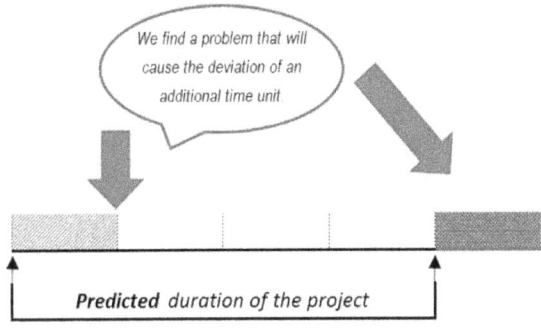

When this takes place, most chiefs, clients and businessmen increase their reserves one time unit as regards costs, and recommend increasing the salary payroll and financial resources to make up for this deviation.

It is completely normal to hear a client requiring us some additions to the project once deals are closed and before starting the project and, it is also normal to have some projects overlapping and originating problems in the organization and performance. I learnt that in life, not every challenge appears in an organized way, one after the other, but that life on the contrary is in itself the overlapping of multiple events. I´ll go on with the example on the chart. The way to see it clearly is by drawing a line that crosses the center of the planning.

We can infer from here that the challenge appeared in the first part of the project. Let´s concentrate on the easiest figures. Do you think that it is the same if a problem arises on the first or on the last day of a period? No, it isn´t the same.

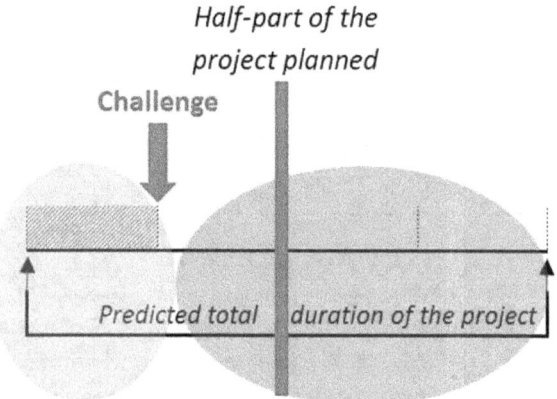

The 75% of the project hasn´t occurred yet, so if at a 25% before finishing it, a deviation of the same characteristics appears ... then ... we have to plan that the remaining time units can also experience a similar deviation.

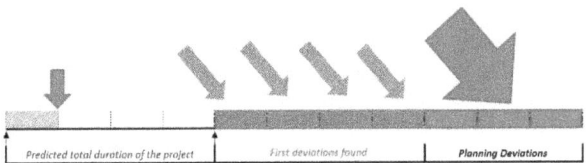

I want to help here, in this book, and with this illustrated experience because I consider that it is one of the best lessons I can share. **When deviations appear in the first part of a project, 80% of the times they are the consequence of bad planning and of the wrong prediction of the requirements.**

So, in the case of a 4-unit-project, we have to add a time unit for each deviation and an additional impact for the 4 deviations. In general a 4-unit-project having problems at the beginning is a problem of 10.3 extra time units.

This is due to the fact that the 75% of the project has not yet been carried out and it is likely to evidence more drawbacks during the fulfillment of the contract.

On the other hand, if the problem appeared in the last 25%, this would mean that the 75%

percent had been carried out as originally planned.

The difference lies in the fact that if problems appear in the first half of a project and we increase resources to avoid the deviation (payroll, materials, shifts); they would have not been enough and challenges would have increased in a highly complex way.

Problems at the beginning of a project are challenges of planning and definition of requirements.
Problems at the end are in general challenges of allocation and planning of resources (human, material and financial).

I have learnt this through experience and, later I got to know that it is an exercise frequently done by executives at multinational companies. I had learnt it by myself at that time, and this lesson had cost me all my savings and I had to work again, after three years, as an employed welder.

I would have liked to know earlier this information I have shared today, but ignoring it at that time, made me what I am now.

I am grateful to life for having learnt on the spot; it gave me the chance to get back on my feet and to write this book to help others.

I thought it was going to be easier. I understood that in life there are happy and sad moments, failures, falls, recoveries, but it is always fundamental **to have the courage to learn and grow.**

Thanks to this courage that appears inside us when we have to make important decisions, I could get back on my feet after the fall. I worked as an employee again, but my salary was not the same as the one I earned when I worked for these international companies.

I worked in a contract for 18 days, and when the job was over, I went back home. Once again, I started to search new possibilities for my start-up and, even if I had failed, I resumed it at full throttle. It was the time to start maturing the way I planned. So I left behind the employee and the entrepreneur was born again. Moreover, I developed the need to learn about planning and strategy.

I went back to giving presentations of the company I have created and more tasks started to be offered to me. My energy was immense and it made me feel that everything was on the right track again.

However, overnight, they changed the chief that allocated tasks at that time and a new one came and with him his own trusted companies.

One day, he called me to a meeting with all the personnel at his company. I had great expectations, I thought this could be the start of a new and better working relationship with him. But, unfortunately, it was not what I had thought. I remember with sorrow, when he told me in front of people from other companies that he didn´t want someone who he did not trust as chief of department.

That day I learnt that a very few people make things easy for those who are outstanding. Frequently, fear takes over insecure people and they choose to eradicate their own fears avoiding the people who generate them. It is difficult to work with someone who knows more than us but it is even more difficult to work with chiefs who know less than us. I went through this many times in my life. There are many bosses and owners that are afraid of those capable of starting their own business. Some bosses just prefer to have a herd of sheep they can dominate at their will, instead of increasing the talent of others. This is plain ignorance; it is usually easier to have followers than leaders below us. I state this with humbleness, but the fact is that I´ve always made a difference due to my curiosity and desire to grow. I did not start a business to overwhelm the others. I started my own business because I wanted to grow and take care of my mother and my beloved ones, with the same strength I had as boy but with the maturity of an adult.

Surprised by this statement and almost immediately, I asked him why he had called me to communicate this to me. He answered that if I wanted to, I could offer myself as a contractor to carry out technical and economic offerings, but that he would NOT assign me any task. Once again a NO in capital letters appeared in my life.

I thanked him for letting me submit estimates, but told him that if those were the conditions, I would not waste my time. So I decided to leave without giving rise to any kind of conflict.

I remember that I got home and I told my wife and I was disappointed again. Even if my working life had always been hard, I had never expected her not to understand the difficult situation I was going through.

I remember that that day I went to bed and it was very difficult to get some sleep for I had to re think once more my working life as regards my decision to start a business of my own.

The first thing I thought was that I had to go over everything again and take new decisions. It wasn´t an easy moment, for I had spent all my savings and I had sold the two plots of land at the same price I had acquired them more than 10 years before. I put the emphasis on the fact that I had played every card to set my own business and what I expected was to see some profits gradually. But I understood once more that life has difficult tests all the time and that if you are willing to carry on, you will have to pay the price.

I started once more to contact the people I had worked with, in deserts and mountain ranges, the same people I had shared important times working outside our area and our homes. I started to study new working alternatives, but all of a sudden a job for Chile turned up. I remember that I arrived at a company, smaller than the one I had started and that I felt completely hopeless. Why did things turn to be like this? I wondered. I noted that sometimes we offer a lot of energy to achieve our goal and that things do not prove to be what we have expected.

I stopped beating around the bush and prepared my test tube to be able to qualify as I had done in my first years. The first thing they asked me was if I could by any chance go through a practice period. So I asked, is this practice period paid? And the answer was that it wasn´t. So, I told them that I would successfully pass the test that same day. I worked from dawn to dusk to demonstrate my professionalism in the field of welding. More than 10 days went by and I asked how much my salary would be and the answer was that I would be paid as much as the other welders. It was then when I asked myself once more why I had to go through this situation if I had been a professional. As a good professional, I committed myself to finish the task. Even if the conditions were quite precarious, I never lost my enthusiasm to complete the duty I had self imposed. Once the task was finished, I prepared my things, bought a ticket, communicated I was leaving and thanked for the opportunity they had given me.

It was then when they recognized my professionalism and the first thing they told me was that they had the option of paying me higher fees. I couldn´t understand why once they had already lost a good worker, they came up with the idea of offering better conditions. On my way back home, I thought that what I had earned was not enough to wait for a month. I had to think again whether I was going to reconsider new alternatives to start a business of my own once more or simply accept the offer I had been made by that company.

I considered it because I didn´t have the capital I had started with and only had a small line of credit with a bank for USD 1000. At that time this amount was not enough even to pay for the salary of a worker. My thoughts became gradually stronger and I made the same question to me over and over again: **What can I do?** I remember that I took a notebook and did exercises in which I asked myself: how can I carry out tasks if I have no money? Then I forced my mind in search of new alternatives. These routines of auto imposed question work started to be fruitful, because I managed to find the answers that gave me self confidence when I needed to introduce the company.

At the time, I had to decide whether I was going to work as an employee at my last job again or I would gather courage again and put my company at their disposal to carry out any project or activity.

I then discovered that magic things start to happen in life when we have an idea and stick to it obsessively.

Before I made my decision, the telephone rang and I received a call from a company that needed to talk to me. It was precisely the company that had offered to set up my company many years before. The first thing I did was to tell them my whole story as from the onset of my company. I was sincere and told them I had no working capital or cash to undertake the tasks they wanted me to carry out. It was then when I saw one of the answers I had written on my notebooks materialize. The answer was: **intent + predisposition = positive result.**

In life, things happen for a reason. I mentioned I had to pay a price and I had already paid it. After all these anecdotes, a new world of possibilities opened up for me and stayed with me for more than 11 running years, for after having lost all the initial capital, I managed to resume the job I had always enjoyed so much. I started to see incredibly good results. Time was not enough to accept the execution of all the projects. I must not forget to mention that growth was experienced in every area of the company. We managed to have staff at our own offices; we had workers manufacturing all our pieces at tremendous facilities we had created ourselves. It really was huge growth.

At that time I thought I had to write about it, that I had to tell my story, even if it was a simple one, I really thought humbly that this story could be useful for many people going through circumstances or situations similar to the ones I had lived and was still living.

Don't be afraid of falling

Resilience

If you are planning to start your own company, always remember that your psychology is the fundamental base.

The origin of a dramatic fall

I write this chapter with the deepest sorrow and pain for having not been able to prevent a huge loss in my life. And now, being an adult, I would like my testimony to help others.

I do not intend to replace the knowledge of people in the health or medicine fields, but I think that these words, coming from someone who has worked all his life, might perhaps help someone.

I therefore, introduce, from my humble point of view, the biggest challenge of all **human beings: our own selves.** We ourselves, out of ignorance, fear or need are prone to become ill.

Life taught me the meaning of a terrible disease suffered by many people, depression. When we are going through it, the levels of a neurotransmitter we have in our brain cells called serotonin drop.

I do not want to replace scientific explanations, but I want to explain that this depression can be increased by an external component. The inability to rest appropriately, sadness, lack of energy, feeling we are not loved or desired, and body pains can represent fatal precedents for people suffering this illness.

Sometimes, we do not realize, but it can improve with a good nutrition, with love, with a feeling of being loved and desired, by feeling useful with an activity that inspires respect and brings us joy, by helping the others, by self programming ourselves to get a good rest. Positive thoughts don´t let serotonin, the hormone of happiness drop.

My wife had a depression called endogenous depression that means, according to the doctors´ explanations that she did not generate the quantities of neurotransmitters necessary to feel well. The fact that it has a genetic origin does not reduce the responsibility we had as a family. Genetics have an influence, but the mind can always allow us to assume a determining role in our destiny. Nothing in this world, as intense as it can be, can take from us the chance of having positive thoughts.

If we are busy, if we have something to do, we will not have time to harbor negative thoughts. We should keep ourselves busy and should always be working for our dreams and desires.

Each person is the owner of its own acts, but in the case of depression, I understand and accept with sorrow, that we sometimes lose the battle and the authority to carry out the activities that help us.

Breaking up a marriage

In the year 2010 I had to take the decision to separate from my wife. Motifs, as specialists explain, come from **both partners** and sadly, each one is a fifty percent accountable for the break up.

I was happy because after 4 years of hard work, I had managed to build a big house with a swimming pool. I remember that at the time, I felt that the two springs it had taken us to build it, had been worth it because we would finally have a nice place to enjoy as a family and which could also contribute to improve our relationship.

Unfortunately, we did not get on well at the time and our children witnessed arguments on a daily basis. There was complete lack of harmony in our life, and this was impaired by my wife´s untreated endogenous depression. We didn´t know this. Nobody is born with all the necessary knowledge, but this does not relieve me of my anger. We many times treat the symptoms but not the cause of our illnesses.

Don't be afraid of falling.
You have to feel complete to have the energy to get back on your feet.
Feeling complete helps the others in the same way as it helps you.

In my case, helping others with their start-ups, gave me the strength to overcome every fall.

After I moved house, I started to read with passion every afternoon until I fell asleep. Viktor Frankl, Lincoln, Freud, Cicerón and tens of authors came to my hands with voracious desire to achieve a more spiritual learning which I´ll simply summarize in two acts: Making contributions and Giving to others.

Never be afraid of making decisions, instead be afraid of not making them.

The loss of two beloved people

Unfortunately on July 12th, 2011 my mother passed away at the age of 83. She had always been the engine of my life. It was a hard moment but, in spite of this, I was pleased as the youngest child who had done the best for her; and this brought peace to my mind. Saying goodbye to one´s parents one day is part of life and, in my case I felt that she had left me when she was elderly and peacefully.

I am writing these words after having taken flowers to her eternal dwelling. To pay tribute to her, I want to include here the quote that accompanies her "*Julia Rosa Gallardo Salinas. Lord, bless the love our mother always gave to us on Earth and let her go on helping us from Heaven*".

I learnt that when a book is written, it is protected for 70 years by intellectual property rights before it enters the public domain forever. Leaving this testimony here, fills me with emotion, because my children will be able to read to my grandchildren about this fantastic lady, not only about the vital importance she had in my life as a mother but as the engine of the great contribution I have made to all those I helped by sharing her lessons.

What caused me terrible sadness at that time was the question my six-year-old son Benjamín asked me. He wanted to know why her granny had passed away. I told him that God had taken her to Heaven with him so that she could rest, after having fulfilled her mission on Earth with us. He asked me why she was in a wooden box; I asked that the body was always placed in a box but that the soul went to Heaven.

Even if painful, I understand that it is normal to say goodbye to our mother when she is an elderly person. But my life turned into a storm when, only two months after that, in September of the same year, my ex wife and mother of my children died the day after her birthday.

This meant very strong and poignant hardships in my life and especially in the life of my children. Sadly enough, her death was the consequence of her illness, which triggered what we knew, could come at any time.

I cannot forget this part of my life as she had blessed me with 3 wonderful children

It was and still is a highly complex situation in the soul of my family and I highlight it in this book of experiences and recommendations, because it also brought about a complex situation in my business.

> *Always act with bravery and courage so that you, your relatives and the people who work with you, workmates and coworkers, always help the others with useful and valued tasks.*

Being engaged in doing something will always give you the strength to wake up the following morning. Sleep well, eat well, use your time wisely and gather positive thoughts.
It is not that difficult. It is only complicated because as we get older we have more issues to deal with.

Supporting my children to help them overcome hard times

Before starting, I would like to say that I have always wanted the best for my three children from the bottom of my heart.

When their mother died, Patricio, the middle child, who was at the time 14 years old, had the worst experience. We found together his deceased mother. And living that situation in his adolescence was extremely hard for him.

Paula, my eldest daughter was finishing university. She then went on getting further degrees and qualifications and became one of the fundamental pillars in my life and my companies. I admire her for her values.

Benjamín, the youngest, was only 6. He had to go through quite a complex process with psychologists and psychiatrists. He was the first one to see parts of this book.

As I have said before, I share this fragment of my history as part of my experience and recommendations because it affected me significantly as far as my business was concerned.

I do not want to focus on my weaknesses, for nothing can be learnt from them, instead I will focus on my strengths. I have always drawn energy from positive thoughts and this is the legacy I want to transmit to my children and to every reader who has this book in his hands.

That year I had to devote 100% to my children and set aside all my business commitments. Together with some health specialists and professionals of child and adolescent mental development, we prepared a scheme so that my children received all the support they needed to overcome the loss and lack of their mother. I committed to this almost exclusively. This was not a minor issue taking into account that my children had lost their mother. I remember a very sad moment, when once I found my son Benjamín inside the wardrobe in fetal position crying. I hugged him strongly and told him what came to my mind at the time. "Son, life is sometimes like this. This is why we have to be strong".

Significant Economic Loss

The following year, the storm had not yet finished in my life, but on the contrary, it started getting wilder. Some suppliers called to warn me of a situation that was taking place in the company: the accounts corresponding to the materials for various projects with different clients and also the manufacturing projects under execution at our premises were not being paid.

One day I unexpectedly went to my company and I felt something weird in the environment. I immediately looked for professionals to intervene the server of the company, and that same night we started to collect all the accounting and financial information of the company. We worked for two weeks to elaborate a general chart of all the expenses and income.

After having finished the final balance, I discovered to my surprise that I was completely broke.

If a coworker does not like something,
he can quit and start again.
An entrepreneur can lose a client and
start with another.
But when an entrepreneur falls, the only
possibility he has to get back on his feet
is by honoring his debts and correcting

his mistakes, even if it takes many years.

At that time I felt I was collapsing in the inside and the outside. What saved me was my determination not to fall because I needed to be the fundamental pillar, in every way, for my three children.

The approximate amount of the loss was 20 million dollars. All this was the consequence of different situations and mismanagement plus anything we can think of related to the loss of such an amount. Do you remember the explanation I included about projects falling behind schedule? Well, something like this had happened to me. It was as if for a project, I had bought tons of steel in excess, and I had doubled the payroll of more than a thousand employees, generating deviations. The result was disastrous. This is why I recommend you re-reading the planning exercise of the previous chapter.

The first thing that came to my mind was something I had learnt some years before, that said that a complex problem had to be divided into smaller problems we could in fact solve. So the first thing I did was to check how much money we had at the time and I paid the smallest suppliers. It is fundamental for a healthy industry to take care of the smallest integrants of the supply chain, because those are hugely impacted by details. The payroll and smallest integrants of the chain go first.

With the biggest suppliers we had to negotiate longer terms, because in a way or in another their size allowed us to negotiate.

This was a very tough period of my life as a businessman, because we had handed out so many checks to pay for materials, inputs and transport that the situation clearly got out of our hands. There came a moment when we did not have any control of the documents that were in the market, and at the same time new documents were being drawn every day.

Cash flow is the most valuable tool of a businessman, because, if collections from clients and payments to suppliers are not coordinated, the impact cannot be possibly imagined.

Most the times we did not have enough cash flow to pay for the documents and thus made us appear in the Commercial Bulletin. The Commercial Bulletin is an entity that publishes a list of people or companies who have not paid their accounts. This affects credits, rates, image, reputation, everything.

I improved all my negotiating skills, because I wanted to solve all the problems, not to avoid them. We talked to our workers and explained simply what had happened and that this would bring about delays of seven days in payments, but that we would always fulfill our duties. They understood and helped patiently and with sacrifice.

We explained that we were going through a crisis and that we would solve it as soon as possible together with our workers. Besides, to calm them down, we had already talked to the personnel and had their understanding and support thanks to the company´s favorable reputation.

In the presence of a crisis, clear and direct communications are fundamental, and to honor the responsibilities undertaken. This generates trust and a better negotiation. Over the years, I saw many people who in front of a crisis hide. Crises are like battles, we have to face them and win them, no matter how long it might take.

It was not only one particular issue; it was the product of years of overlooked details, which together constituted a mountain of problems. I had to start making deals with banks, with financial entities, and many other agreements to be able to go on working. To keep on working was the only way of paying our duties, which were not minor.

It was there that I became an expert at dealing with complex and adverse situations and at developing strategies and negotiation.

Never give up

Empower your Inner Strength.
Your thoughts are vital to reinforce yourself
psychologically every day.

Starting to make the company steady

As regards my personal life, I had to rely on people who helped me with the house chores, and my children´s support, but I had to be present when they attended their psychological and psychiatric sessions.

As regards the company, apart from seeking new working alternatives, I had to increase my invoicing to face the huge deficit I was going through.

Believe me, it was not an easy period of my life, I had to be a mother and a father at the same time and to lead a company that had managed to hire 1500 workers in a few months.

What have always prompted me into action are my children, the desire to overcome complex situations and prove myself I have the ability and determination to leave crises behind.

It is important not to make problems bigger than what they really are; our energy must be applied to making them smaller and strengthening opportunities.

We mustn´t feel this as a weakness or threat, but as the opportunity to test our strength.

In the face of uncertainty, we should ask ourselves how to get out of it. I remember that during our holidays in 2013, my youngest son Benjamín went away with her sister Paula and my grandson Vicente to Disney in Orlando, Florida. Benjamín brought as a present for me, a book with a red cover, entitled Think and Become Rich, by Napoleón Hill. He told me, father, I apologize for not giving you a bigger present. I told him how grateful I was, because his thoughts were focused on helping his father.

The book deals extensively with the importance of the brain and thoughts as the most valuable treasures that help you create everything your mind can achieve or it can simply act as an antidote against failure, as it doesn´t accept a NO for an answer.

This book represented a very important landmark, since from then on, I started to listen to audio books when I went to the supermarket with my children, when we went out or when I attended meetings for new businesses or projects. As I spent a lot of my time in the car, this proved to be a powerful tool against failure.

I started to listen to different audio books regularly and my passion for reading increased. I matured the power of words and I started to build different ideas to help me in difficult times. I could reinforce continuously my attitude and my skills and find the strength to move on.

During that time I improved my life quite a lot and I concentrated 100% on paying my debts and having a positive attitude at all times and trying to find things that brought me joy; I had to show my little son, that in life, even if it can be hard, we must move on.

I thanked the people that had trusted me and who are still working for my company. **There are no mistakes, but tests, to change the way you are doing things and to move on to the next stage.**

I saw that the next stage would be an improved version of me as regards every aspect of my life, trying to find the way to help many people.

I started to dream again, and to believe that once I had left all my nightmares behind, I would be able to think differently and more efficiently. I would like to have enough time, and I`ve already expressed this desire in writing, to create an Academy to train people in different jobs such as welding, mechanics and other fields and also in soft skills to complement people´s working and personal lives.

To be sincere, at that time I was always pending on my telephone and connected 24 hours a day, the 365 days of the year. Even if I went out with my children at weekends, I had to be constantly checking all the possible obstacles that could appear in the execution of each of the company´s projects.

I did not value my time, as all those who claim not to have enough time. For this reason, I have always considered that entrepreneurs, should one day, enter the world of personal development and growth.

Challenges once the company is steady

The years that follow 2011 and 2012, which I consider the most difficult years of my life, were a period of immense effort and sacrifice to make the company steady.

We had got to the point in which our finances were already under control, we did not have big problems with the banks, providers or financial entities. We were seeing again the light that had disappeared in the past, and we even managed to view the path again and started to think how to shed light to our journey from then on.

I want to share one anecdote. Once we were carrying out maintenance tasks at a plant that were supposed to last for 15 days. In 2014 I had to accompany my son Benjamín to his medical appointments. A client phoned me to tell me that there were problems with the execution of a project and we were not meeting the committed deadline. The project had to be finished by 12 that evening.

I went immediately to the client`s premises. I talked with the main leaders of the company and promised to reverse the situation. However, I asked them to let me have a talk with everybody and I invited them to listen to my conversations if they wanted to.

I called all my company leaders and asked them to gather all the staff and buy lots of soft drinks for everybody. Firstly, I greeted them one by one; I explained the situation and told them we had lost control of the equipment maintenance we were carrying out. I also told them that I believed in them and that I could also understand their tiredness and frustration because things were not going as planned. I also explained this maintenance was of the utmost importance for the company because it had been more than 4 years since we last performed a maintenance project with this client.

I also mentioned that in spite of all the difficulties, I trusted them and I was sure they could change the situation dramatically in our favor and stated that it was very important to challenge ourselves and fulfill our undertaking. I was aware that it required a great effort, but I was also convinced we could finish our job at 00:00 that night.

All of them started nodding, understanding which the problem was. I told them that I also had problems, that I was a human being as all of them, that I had had to interrupt the appointment with my son´s doctor due to the problems I had with this project. I also told them I was a father and a mother at the same time and that I perfectly well understood any of them going through the same situation. Then I said: "You, all of you highly experienced workers, please tell me which would be THE BEST IDEA". People listened to me and responded consequently. I could see them working with determination and enthusiasm and we managed to revert the unfavorable situation. When we finished, people could hardly realize that within 24 hours we had finished the job, and the client could not believe that with this attitude we had achieved to solve the problems, provide an answer and finish the job in 24 hours.

Attitude generates strength and I think this anecdote will be useful for many people, because we all need each other, we can all have problems, but with team spirit we can get what we want, even solve a complex situation that seems to be lost, and in 24 hours! I remember that I have asked our client to let us work, to stop pressing us for those 24 hours. On many occasions the impatience of the client causes delays, but don´t get confused, it is beneficial to be under the client´s pressure. Without this pressure, we would be bored, we wouldn´t compete to improve.

At that time, I could hardly realize that I had empowered more than 300 workers in both shifts. They joined as they arrived and with enthusiasm and energy we managed to change completely the negative results we had had so far.

That was a huge achievement as we could fulfill an objective that appeared to be impossible to reach.

A new challenge

In 2015 all our financial and economic inconveniences had been solved; we had already fulfilled all the duties we had undertaken due to the severe drawbacks experienced from 2011 to 2012. We were relatively calm, as the financial situation of our companies was stable and we were growing again. We started to diversify into different items and at the same time, we kept on growing as far as infrastructure was concerned. I had transformed the organization into a 12-company-holding. Why do we diversify? To minimize risk.

Life had taught me that I had to keep on growing and learning; and a challenge was waiting for me to teach me the second most important lesson which is for me, to have positive thinking: **"always have the right documents at hand and do it before it is required"**.

After having experienced all these difficult family and financial times, and once we were quite reorganized with our 12 companies, we undertook a project pretty important because of the deadline we had to meet.

The execution project brought serious economic problems to the company: we had undertaken a project for a period of four months, for an amount of approximately 10 million dollars.

We started the project at full throttle and we had shifts working day and night both at our premises as well as at the client´s location where the works were being carried out.

As we were moving forward, we happened to encounter many drawbacks, among them that the pieces we had manufactured according to the plans did not coincide at the assembly stage. That is to say that our plans did not coincide with the reality and so the pieces did not coincide with the layouts at the places where the original assembly had to be carried out. We couldn´t understand how that could have happened. We did some research, and found out that there had been several modifications and that they had not informed us while we were manufacturing the pieces. They had changed the scale model 18 times before the assembly!

Let´s bear this in mind, if we fail in the plans, the communications and the logistics, the battle will be absolutely lost. Even with optimism, if we don´t support our work with timely accurate documents or don´t get every day a signature to support deviations, YOU WILL LOSE.

The plans and changes in the models were not the only problems; they had to provide us with equipment and they had not even bought them. This caused a chain of events of non synchronicity with the other contractors who had delivered the structures assembly late, causing in turn a delay in our assembly of the manufactured pieces. This did not let us move forward and, we had many inconveniences with the 13 companies with which we were interacting in the different disciplines.

When the deadline was reached we had already manufactured every piece and did not have more than 30% of the project assembled.

An adverse storm that had originated due to the bad use of the master program in the hands of the company responsible for the execution of the project called EPCM. This acronym stands for the English words Engineering, Procurement, Construction, and Management. This had not been properly carried out by the previous engineering company. A project has a concrete plan and objective, and a program is the combination of tens or hundreds of entries of each specialty. The combination of problems makes prevention impossible as they are all planning problems.

Once again I had to negotiate and try to solve these inconveniences as I could.

We explained the situation, we told them all the problems we had to execute the project, and that as a company it was very important for us to be able to finish our manufacturing and assembly projects.

We also explained that we had always solved any inconvenience in projects in the course of their execution with our clients. They answered that there would be no problem with them as a company, that they would respect all that had to be paid, but they wanted us to find a way to finish the project.

We trusted them and thought they were serious clients for a simple reason: they used to work for the great Chilean mining industry and for the entire world. We thought we would have no inconveniences with them. My advice is that we have to rely more on our documents than on our perception. Due to this confidence, we went on with the project, making the necessary changes, until in October 2015, we had to resume our conversations to settle a part of the costs that had already exceeded the estimated and approved amount.

It was then when we found that at first they had said there would be no problem with the inconveniences, and later on they started to resist negotiations. We had financed ourselves for more than four months so far and we had more than 500 people working.

From then on, problems started to appear one after the other. In fact, they suggested we file a complaint with the trade chamber in Santiago.

We did not want to abandon the work and we started to finance with other contracts until we got to December and we finally filed a complaint for more than 15 million dollars, subject to increases, and asking for mediation. A 4-month-project was finally finished in 14 months. What was really sad was that we had only estimated four months for the entire project.

Once more I found myself trying to see a way to overcome the economic problem after the project, experiencing again the same economic hardships, but in a different way because we thought that the clients we had been working for would fulfill their duties.

We could have had far smaller costs to finish the project, but when there are delays costs do not only increase but multiply.

Once more we had to go through a situation similar to the one in 2012, when I was forced to elaborate financing plans with banks, suppliers, financial entities and on top of it, we had to deal with the contraction of all the mining projects due to the price of copper. That was a hard blow for we had to face factors external to our company. I thought at that moment that the situation was going to be extremely difficult due to the status of the economy and in fact, I was not wrong.

I then focused on reversing the situation. After what had happened I could only think how to keep the company alive, to go on honoring my debts and how I would deal with something that was completely new for me. I had no experience in this type of negotiation called mediation and I really doubted the result of the mediation would be fair.

In the face of the circumstances, I could only try to encourage myself, I stopped for a while to think and I told myself "I have to go on expanding the company within the national territory".

I had to find new alternatives to increase my invoicing so that my profit margin could afford the costs of the loss that project had caused to the company, the payment of debts and on top of that, the cost of mediation, lawyers, etc, which I considered illogical and unfair.

If one day you consider going through mediation, I´ll give you some good advice: make sure you have clear documents before the process.

We went through the mediation process for over 3 years, with all the inconveniences it caused. It was quite a complicated process as we had to reconstruct the whole story. Arbitration entails a thorough accounting and operative audit and this implied explaining in detail from the very beginning when we had been invited to participate up to the completion of the whole project.

There was a great deal of information to be gathered and explained to the lawyers that participated in the whole process. We had to go over it many times, lots of abnormal things happened, that was why we had to change lawyers more than once. For this reason, I had to travel to Santiago almost every day as we had to meet with the lawyers. We wasted these years going to meetings with lawyers to prepare the hearings resulting from that famous mediation, which was done to fit big companies.

We spent several years from meeting to meeting and we wasted precious time due to the lack of effective communication.

We spent over three years with a mediation that provided negative results for the company. This process not only brought about economic losses but physical and psychological hardships for all those who had been involved. Knowing that we were just waiting to be paid for what we had already paid as a direct cost of the project, with no profit whatsoever, was really devastating.

We just wanted to recover what we had spent in the project that had been completed and the results of which were evident. News were still worse when in May 2019, we were told that we had lost in the Chamber of Trade in Santiago, in the Court of Appeals and in the Supreme Court. That´s to say, that none of the instances had ruled in our favor.

I could never understand how, even in the presence of clear documents that had been audited by an expert appointed by the same mediator and, who had also determined that everything we had done as regards technical issues and documentation was right, we got that result from the mediation which had been unilaterally reached by the mediator. After having obtained a favorable result on the part of the experts, the judge dismissed their conclusions and decided we had lost that famous mediation. That was unfair, for we could have at least reached a compromise, as we had been forced to lower the amounts significantly.

We ended up with a loss of 13 million dollars as a consequence of the required reduction and they finally did not even pay for the project that had been already finished and in operation.

I found myself thinking once more how to recalculate and manage to overcome the crisis. Many times we think things will never be the same, because we have already gone through them and we experience anguish and nostalgia.

However, I have always thought and will think for the rest of my life that we have to struggle, and go back at full throttle, with all the force we can draw from ourselves. It was then that I started to fill myself with positive thoughts. And I started to tell myself: "I have to diversify much more the services for the industry", I have to look for new alternatives to increase invoices levels", "and I have to concentrate on keeping my company steady, each month, to be able to afford salaries, my duties with suppliers and also to find the way to keep on growing.

The only purpose we need to have in our lives is the will to do things, the strength to keep on fighting instead of just seeing how things get worse and worse. Do not let yourself be depressed, do not go to bed. Problems won´t be solved spontaneously by them.

Life gives you the chance to plan everything again every day. I suggest this as a way of living and I really enjoy getting the people in my company involved.

I had paid my debts once more. It is fundamental to assume our responsibilities. We must have inner positive thinking and the absolute conviction that we can achieve things.

It is always fundamental to have complete control of our lives and the desire to overcome difficulties and to be 100% convinced that with courage we will make our dreams and wishes come true.

Grow

Understanding the system

GROW

Expanding and diversifying in the mining industry

This is my mission, but not only in Chile. I want to help my country exporting my services to bring businesses to our nation.

I like diversifying in the industry, and I have proved so, as we have been always expanding. We have constantly created new businesses that allowed us to go on growing while we concentrated on maintaining our reputation throughout the history of our company.

At the time I am writing this book, the company I represent is entering the world of industrial maintenance. This represents a world of possibilities: mechanical and structural maintenance, repair of mining equipment and equipment assembly. Likewise, we possess a tremendous infrastructure to support the contracts with a collection of machines and equipment that allows us to manufacture pieces that are not commercialized and with a 24-hour service the 365 days of the year. This simply seeks to focus our service on differentiation and innovation.

I say this with respect, because we struggle with us and against us to be better and find the way to overcome problems, cross frontiers and we do not just want to be good. We want to be the best; we want recognition, not only in our country but in the rest of the world.

For this reason, it is fundamental for entrepreneurs to be aware that being good is not enough; we have to be the best in our jobs.

GROW

A different way to see life

In 2017, I started to attend conferences in my country accompanied by my son Benjamín. Then, I went on looking for new alternatives and last year I did some courses on High Performance Reading where I met really special people.

Since then and for almost 2 years now, I have started a journey of personal growth and I have not stopped having different training not only in Chile but also in the United States and Europe.

I have met very important people in the field of personal growth and this gave me a broader view of change.

Today I understand more than ever that to manage change the most important thing is to know where to go and to coordinate my expectations with those of the people around me, my family and employees. Change is based on clear communication and on training everybody in change.

I started growth based on how I want to live my life, and it was then that I conceived the idea of this book of experiences and suggestions.

We, as human beings are full of internal powers, and a fundamental one is courage. With courage we can change our whole life if we have clear and sound objectives.

Make Contributions

The highest achievement in life is GIVING

My experience with Tony Robbins

(Based on The 6 needs of the Human Being. Unleash The Power Within. Tony Robbins)

In 2018 I attended for the first time one of Tony Robbins´s events at Nueva York in the United States. Tony Robbins´s mentor was none other than Jim Rohn.

Among dozens of important people, he trained more than 40 million people in more than 100 countries and the total invoicing of all his companies amounts to 5,500 thousand million dollars per year from his 55-company-holding. What Robbins has done over the years is admired by many people and undoubtedly by me. I have felt identified with his story, which even if different from mine, should be highlighted as it is the clear example that dreams can come true.

His main lesson states that the reason why people do not make progress is because of fear, and that this fear originates from six human needs. People concentrate on what they need and, when they cannot satisfy these needs, they get paralyzed.

Here I would like to share what I have learnt but in my own words, as I know that many of you might not know what Robbins´ trainings are about. Let me share then part of a 50-hour-training I received in 4 days

The Need of Certainty.

Generally, people need the certainty of being healthy, wealthy, of having a permanent job and of being heard. Without these certainties, they cannot move forward. We can identify them with the phrase: "if I had xxxx", replacing these xxxx for any spiritual, physical or economic asset they certainly want. With these certainties, we are thought to be able to do anything we wish.

Example: *If my accounts were settled, I could be at peace and grow, but as I cannot make ends meet at the end of the month, I live in constant concern.*

But this is not the only need we have to satisfy as human beings. There are many more.

The Need of Variety.

This need is also related to uncertainty. Without variety we grow bored and indifferent. We need variety and uncertainty to grow. These are the complements of people who need certainty. They need more clients to feel realized. They look for variety in clients and products to grow; they are not satisfied with only one client. We identify them with the phrase … "if I had xxxx".

Example: *If I had more clients, I could grow.*

The Need to feel important.

This need is related to the emotions of wanting to be heard, accepted and respected.

Example: *when I am promoted, I will be able to take better care of my family. When I earn more money (feeling we are worth more), I will grow.*

According to Tony Robbins, we all have 3 needs, without exception, to a smaller or bigger extent, and with these 3 needs we start working dependently or independently trying to develop value.

But even then, people experience a huge void; years go by and they do not grow. Even if they have been able to amass a big fortune, they feel they need more money, more variety, more acceptance and respect from the others to fill that void.

Years go by, they accumulate more and more, and the void never fills. They hire people and they share with them their need of certainties, their need of variety, their need to feel important, and they do not move forward; neither them, nor the people they hire or help and consequently, clients do not grow either.

What really happens is that there are other 3 needs much more important, the needs we always want to develop and possess "after" the 3 first needs. They are:

The Need to feel connected.

This is the need to love and feel loved, to want someone and feel wanted; the need to connect.

Nobody wants to work alone. Everybody wants to work with somebody else, to have friends, a partner, working partners and working communities.

Example: thanks to the reciprocal love and respect of my mother I can connect.

The Need to grow.

This need is fundamental. If I do not grow, I die. There is no chance of standing still. If I don´t move forward, then I´ll move backwards.

This is what happens to people who don´t grow, who don´t learn or understand the others.

Example: I will grow when such and such a thing happen, meanwhile I keep on waiting. If I wait, I´ll paralyze, I´ll become stagnant, I´ll go backwards. If I prompt action, I´ll move forward.

The Need to make contributions or Give

All of us need to help the others, because helping others to grow helps us grow too as human beings. If we don´t help the others, we won´t grow.

Example: I´ll help once I have first settled my accounts. I´ll buy an expensive ticket when I have the money. When I have money, I´ll help the others.

What usually happens is that we think that if we start satisfying the first 3 needs, then we will be able to satisfy the next 3, but on the other hand, just the opposite happens!

Only by satisfying the second 3 needs, will we be able to start satisfying the first 3.

I thank my mother, who insisted on that order: giving, growing and connecting.

<u>In the business world we have to give, do, grow and connect with our clients.</u>

Only when we are decided to grow, will we achieve it. When excuses disappear, when the Parkinson law, which establishes that we always use 100% of our time disappears, we are really able to take off.

Only when we make contributions, does the universe start contributing with us.

MAKE CONTRIBUTIONS

In short, only when we help others grow, when we pay attention to them, when we understand them, will we create the path to our growth and get the others' attention and understanding.

I do not believe in time or monetary charity. I only believe that we have to work to grow and help others grow, being helpful, welding the parts that need to be welded.

Suggestions for entrepreneurs

As I have stated before, the idea of this book sprang from my vast experience and uninterrupted learning. "I want my children as adults to know the experiences and recommendations that were important for me when starting a new job.

For this book to serve as a really useful guide and encourage meritocracy, the first questions I asked myself were: Who am I writing this book for? For my children, for entrepreneurs? For those who want to be entrepreneurs? Perhaps for government officials, so that they stop working for the short term and stop saying that this or that is not possible? And the truth is that I am writing it for all of them.

How can it be useful for them? Undoubtedly by reading it and sharing their opinions with their peers and workmates.

But remember: what is perfect is the enemy of what is good, because perfection is a path not an event. Everything can be made perfect day after day, what is healthy is to concentrate on what is positive and not negative. If what we do is 98% right, the remaining 2% is just the chance to improve. I then, invite you to concentrate on your 98% of courage and commitment.

We have the whole life ahead of us to improve and, there is where the beauty of life will be found.

Remember that the path is the only thing we have. Fill your path with your own light and shed light on the path of the others.

Don´t forget that the search for perfection is the most innocent path to auto boycotting because it does not let us enjoy our imperfect humanity.

Having a dream is the first requirement

Having dreams is the base of everything

Firstly, I would like to talk about the importance of dreams. And I say, dreams, not wishes. Dreams can be more specific and dreams are nebulous; you may want to have a car or to fall in love.

But when we start something with all our heart, we need to have a concrete dream. When you really want to start your own business and you have already identified your dream, you only have to ask yourself, do you really imagine yourself fulfilling your dream? Do you picture yourself in 1, 5, and 10 or 20 years with the same dream, living it, enjoying it, even if you know it won´t be easy?Many people think that being a businessman means to be focused on results, on how to generate profit, create strategies, talk about marketing, sales, etc. Of course all these are all right, but they are only useful when they are framed inside a dream.

The dream is the engine and union of all the rest. Having a dream and fulfilling it are very different things. It is possible to dream and to be happy just dreaming, or it is possible to dream and not to be able to wait for the day to break to make it come true.

How important is it for you to be able to do everyday what you really like? To be a real entrepreneur you have to belong to the group of people who cannot wait till the other day to get started. We, businessmen, really take our dreams seriously.

Finding the time is the first step

People say they have no time, but they have to make time!

The answer is simple (like most of the solutions of complex problems). Firstly, we need to save some of our daily time to plan better.

We start by learning that a change of perspective supposes a change in the way we see subjects. We will have a new approach, a new point of view, something to be observed from a different angle. Something that will certainly urge us to devote some time to think about the actions we will have to take.

If you ask somebody in a meeting to turn off the light, he will instinctively look at the walls to find the switch, and will then try to press it to turn the light on or off.

Depending on how time for improvements is organized, you will be able to move forward. Your will is not enough, it will also depend on your personal interests and daily activities. Now we have the useful tool of investigating on the internet. In this way you devote your time to do it, but it is advisable to think first what you need and not to go directly to the solution. When I started, internet didn´t exist. I would have saved a lot of time and money. In my times, the searcher by excellence was the dictionary.

I remember that being a very little child there was an album called THE WORLD OF WHY. We used to buy the colored sheets and stick them. One of them, for example asked: why do planes fly? Soon afterwards, the answer was released and like this, questions and answers appeared one after the other.

Nowadays, before searching on the internet, we should pose the question HOW, how can I do this? How can I do this other thing? HOW CAN I MAKE MY DREAMS COME TRUE?

The key lies in working out our minds on a constant basis, and asking ourselves all the necessary questions and looking for all the necessary answers. For a simple reason, the mind works in search of different alternatives, and if you force it to provide them, it will go after the answers. We should take into account that we always have to write down all our questions and then we come up with three answers for each question. Now, we could go deeper and apply a multiple of 30 for each question, this will certainly represent going very deeply into our thoughts and finding the answer we need. The idea is that we could carry out these processes with a system created by ourselves and we should be able to do it within the minimum lapse of time. In this way, we will be able to make our mind work at a good speed and in time, we will become a person who can find answers before any other person who does not train this technique.

Attitude - Certainty

You need to add intention and certainty to everything you do; this will shed light on your path towards achievement.

What does being certain mean? Being certain means, for example, that when I wake up early and have to carry out any activity, my objective will be clear and I will make plans with the full conviction that I will be able to finish what I need to do.

I remember one occasion when a client needed my services. At that time, I wasn´t an entrepreneur yet, I was just a welder and a client called me to perform a job. This job consisted in repairing a boiler tube. For those who do not know, a boiler is a power source that generates high pressure vapor which in turn generates energy that can be used in different machines, equipment or processes.

The job consisted in repairing a pipe in the roof of a huge boiler, the functioning of which had only been interrupted to carry out these repairs. As it had only been stopped to carry out repairs, it was terribly hot with a temperature of approximately 50° and the welding was at the level of the head of the person who had to do the welding. I remember that when I went up to have a look at the job to be done, I invited a friend and told him I had to do the job urgently. We had to allocate a real time to the job and be extremely concrete when talking to the client and telling him we would do the job within a predetermined lapse of time. We talked to the client and the first thing he asked me was how long the repair works would take. We would take 3 hours to complete the repairs, to which he answered that I was offering a very short time to carry them out. Without any hesitation, I answered that that was the right time and it finally took us 2 hours and 40 minutes, less than the time suggested. This is what we call certainty.

When intent is certain, it becomes determination, and determination is the path that will lead you to the fulfillment of your goals.

When you are thinking of carrying out an activity that might generate dividends to make your living, materialize your dreams or afford a different life, determination is vital.

The path has to be clearly spotted beforehand, and once it is visualized, follow it straightaway.

Don´t look backwards or side wards, just look ahead. We can determine your life only if we focus where the objective is. This can be compared with target shooting, if you want to hit the target you have to think constantly in the point. And each time you make focus on something you also have to focus on your thoughts of what you want to be or where you want to get to. Your whole life is full of possibilities that only you can materialize. This is what we have to aim at with all our determination, with all our strength, with all our heart. This is precisely what I refer to when I speak about determination; to make use of what it takes to achieve all the promises you have made to yourself without setting limits to your determination. For this reason looking only ahead will help you overcome the obstacles to get where your determination wants to get.

Transform your determination in a reality so that one day in the future you can say "I challenged myself and when the moment came, I didn´t hesitate. Even if I had many drawbacks on my journey, I never thought I would not make it".

When you challenge yourself you need the courage to persevere to reach your objective. This requires sound determination and discipline to overcome problems and crises. Always remember that you are in full control of your life and your thoughts and when you have decided what you want to do or be in life, you will have to keep on focusing your determination on your defined objective. And the stronger your desire is, the sooner you will fulfill what you decided to fulfill in your life. Always remember to focus on your determined objective because this will help you achieve your determination, the one you had when you told yourself "I will struggle, whatever it takes, to fulfill my purpose". This will dictate how you go through this life.

Consider that many people wait for miracles to occur, today more than ever before, miracles can really happen simply through determination and discipline.

The beginning of the day

We have to start our days with high spirits and full of energy.

It is fundamental to start our day in the right way, many people start in a bad humor. This doesn´t help, on the contrary. We have to take full advantage of every morning. Fill yourself with positive thoughts. Positive thoughts are the foundations of identity.

Identify the others´ talents, the positive side of the others. Eliminate completely of your life the "I can´t", "I don´t see" and "I don´t want". Dream of big projects. It is not important if they don´t turn out to be good at first.

It is essential to know that when we start our day, due to the things that might have happened we feel we have no strength or spirits but, there is an objective to follow and we need to the drive to move on, even if it is complicated, even if we are going through tough situations.

It only takes to apply your energy, to really want it, to guide yourself with an attitude that, in presence of negative thoughts, can counterbalance them with positive energy and with all the strength you can give to each task you perform.

Remember that life is here and now. Don´t let your negative feelings outdo your energy. This energy is first and is the main engine to achieve what you want in life.

Commitment

Commit to doing small changes every day and over the years you will see the results.

Big achievements take time. Be patient.

Talking with efficient people will save your time and resources.

Avoid theoretical people incapable of working with experienced people.

Avoid boring presentations that will end up confusing you as regards the advantages or disadvantages of circumstances and situations.

Ask for examples that suit your requirements.

Our job allows us for a while, to imagine the future, but bear in mind that we live TODAY. We have to understand what we can do TODAY. It is useful to be told about the future, but not excessively. Many books deal better with the subject of the future than with the meeting being held. Commit to the project.

The best example, if you want to understand a requirement, is to ask: which is the real need? And what do you need it for?

If in front of you, you find experienced coworkers and clients eager to explain a problem or a solution, take advantage of them. It is the base of commitment.

Trust

We must be self-confident, considering that, if things do not prove to be as we wished, we can try again.

Self-confidence and trust are an invaluable set of tools.

Trust is built mainly talking to the people that are around us and also to those who are constantly cooperating with your businesses. And what is fundamental is to explain where they have to put the focus on your business, letting them know clearly what your company is doing and where it needs to get to, that´s to say, its objective. Then, when we get people involved, they automatically start feeling closer to us, they start trusting us. This closeness enables us to indicate, if we have fallen behind in a project, that we need their cooperation. Like this, people have the opportunity to show trust through commitment.

Trust, communication and commitment form a triangle that causes synergy and transforms into a circle, and this in turn, becomes beneficial for all those who apply this formula.

Beliefs

You have to find the way to exterminate negative beliefs.

"I am like this", "I was taught like this", etc., are negative phrases and beliefs. We see a girl and a boy and we refer to the boy as the strongest. We shouldn´t have limiting beliefs. All our beliefs should be enabling beliefs.

I would like to add something. I generally hear people saying that the one who has a good idea can achieve great things. Let me disagree. A good idea is not necessary. **It is necessary to know how to work on ideas**. There are thousands of ideas, but just a few know how to implement them. In short, it is not about having an idea; it is about creating the conditions to turn them into facts.

It is also important to take into account that when you limit yourself, you don´t let your brain expand and search for other alternatives.

When we work convinced that the idea we have is the best, even if we cannot implement it, we will finally understand why we failed. This will be our great lesson to improve and try again and again until we manage to find the final solution.

Determination

If we think things will be easy, they will turn up to be difficult ... but if we act with the certainty of succeeding, this will undoubtedly happen.

The determination or self conviction that we will achieve something gives us extra energy. Sometimes it is a slight boost of confidence and others the antidote against failure. Determination means not to quit. It means to be clear about what we to do and do it, always finding the way not to surrender and get to the end.

Determination has to be there, even when we know it is not going to be easy, that we will find many obstacles, problems and falls. It is your conviction and the commitment not to quit what builds the determination that you will get your objective.

It is not the same as certainty, because certainty is related to organization; it means to be well organized, for example, when we say that we are going to do something in two days, two months or in whichever time and we organize the resources to do so.

Once we were carrying out a project which appeared to be unprofitable but, somehow, we promised ourselves to finish it. At the same time, we were working for a multinational company in a big, but on a tight budget. The project was carried out perfectly well. As a consequence of this, a client who had seen us working realized that the company they had hired was not the one carrying out the task, but us. This project did not give us important profit because we worked as subcontract. However, we were the ones that had created the project and the company that collected the profits was the one that had sold it.

You can also become a company that resells projects, mainly for big companies. This gives very good results if your service is efficient. Nowadays, big companies need to have service providers that can help them solve their requirements or needs as soon as possible.

After two years, the final client directly looked for us for a really important project. He required an estimate directly to us and also to our former client, who eventually was the intermediary. For this project, we estimated the work in 2 million dollars and 7 days of work, while our competitor, for whom we had already carried out similar projects, estimated 2, 5 million dollars and a term of 45 days. We won the bid, carried out our job impeccably and strengthened our reputation.

It meant for us huge profits as far as credibility is concerned and this generated a new client, who at present, still believes in our commitment with objectives.

Discipline

Discipline is the continuous development of an improved version of you. Bear in mind that discipline in new businesses is the strength you need to move on to the next stage you want to reach.

Being disciplined means to understand that we all have the same 24 hours to perform an activity, and that the use of these 24 hours in an organized and disciplined way transforms these 24 hours in productive goals.

Prepare yourself for meetings with clients. Study closely your questions before posing them. Study the people who attend.

Effective people are those responsible for unmasking the chain of contradictions within a project. They are responsible for carrying out the project properly and timely.

Try to understand gestures, explanations. Ask them which have been the critical success factors they had in the past, and which are their most common successes and failures. Learn from them.

Do not just rely on complex spreadsheets, visit working sites, talk to the staff who, according to their experience will make interesting contributions and understand what people know, need and feel.

I remember an anecdote in which one coworker was afraid. The project was very important and the client was very enthusiastic. The meeting room was ready, everything planned days before. It was going to be the conclusion of some great deals. I don´t know if for everyone, but it was very important indeed for the client and the worker. Everything he desired depended on this sale. For the client it was also important as it meant a slight progress in the project.

The time of the meeting finally came and the financial divisions of both companies were present, everything was ready for the negotiation.

The meeting started, but something was not working properly.

The client was uncomfortable, even when the information and important advantages of the project were evident, something was wrong.

Finally it happened. The first part in which the scope of the project was discussed finished. The second part followed, the big challenge: the negotiation.

The client started to evidence uneasiness, he did not like anything at all; even when he was offered a special discount he showed no enthusiasm. He was still interested, but he appeared to be angry.

To save face, he stayed for a second meeting to settle the conditions of the deal. But the client behaved in a strange way. Sometime later, the client´s wife asked him that night: "*Darling, how have things gone today?*", and the answer was as unfortunate as his claim "*Darling, you have no idea how terribly uncomfortable I felt. For over an hour I had to hear about lots of issues that would benefit my company, but as I did not know the price, I couldn´t make any of the questions I was interested in. I was only worried about the price. The company shareholders had been very clear to me. If I did not get a good price, I had to introduce other items in the negotiation. The seller kept me for an hour close to a heart attack and when he finally told me the price I had no chance of asking about the scope of the solution, because it was already late to start clearing my doubts. I hope to have my opportunity in the second meeting to establish my criteria in the negotiation. I´d better go to bed now, tomorrow it will be a different day*".

From this experience I learnt the importance of explaining the price framework from the very beginning. This helps throughout the negotiation because it settles the working horizon. Do not move forward with your clients if you do not agree on the prices.

Tell the prices at the beginning of the meeting. This will help the meeting to be more fluent and productive. Knowing the prices, meetings are more interesting, there are more questions and more trust and empathy are generated.

Besides, always consider that the best negotiation is the one in which both parties win. Sometimes you may have a high value, but if you manage to satisfy the client´s needs, he would not oppose to your offer. The reason is simple, he will be sure you will comply with your duties.

Leadership

You are the captain that guides your life and thoughts.

Control your destiny; do not let the others do it for you.

Leadership is, in a few words, the ability to get close to people. This leadership is created basically with direct, clear and honest communication, which will in turn get people together giving them the message you want to transmit and consequently being fully understood.

Good leadership requires transmitting ideas and actions from the heart, using simple, actual and concrete terminology. This leadership becomes highly effective because it is based on honesty. When you transmit from your heart, people open up and expand to follow your thoughts, your advice, your proposal, your strategies, your vision and your example.

Always consider that the leader must be the person who sets the example. You cannot let people down because you will lose their credibility. This is very similar to couple relationships. If you lose trust, even if you do your best to recover it, the relationship will never be the same. Pay attention to transmit trust, seriousness and sincerity and act as a true leader.

Optimism

We should have an optimistic attitude to face the problems we encounter in life.

No doubt, the number 1 lesson I recommend is to have a positive mindset. It helps find the "how" to solve any situation, even the hardest one.

Look for people who value their own knowledge and the knowledge of others, people who are tolerant and flexible and who enjoy working in teams. We should not surround ourselves with people who do not cooperate or who do not listen to the others, who only want to be heard and are not willing to cooperate at work or work with teams.

Positive attracts positive while negative attracts negative. Attraction concepts have been dealt with by numerous books I have read, but here I will share my experience so that you can be surrounded by the right people.

There are no perfect human beings, that´s why it is important to understand how to gather good working teams, and for this we have to work in full accordance with other people.

Thinking about dreams is thinking big. To implement them is a constant process that never ends, that is the reason why successful people are always looking for ways to increase their success.

With this example I am going to include, I want you not to make the same mistake I did. I have met people, I don´t know if by chance, who are successful in their business and think that their lives have reached the maximum potential and that nothing or nobody can stop them. They then started to spend their money lavishly, firstly convinced that they were satisfying their personal desires through luxurious items and things that did not represent added value to their needs. For example, they rent an expensive house and as they cannot afford the high costs, are continuously in debt and pretend to be what they are not really. It must be noted that many books and audio books teach us that we have to be and pretend. They never say that you have to acquire debts, but that you have to find the ways to be able to do the things you intend to do.

My experience when my income started to grow was the following: I lived in a small 42-meter flat with my family and rented a small warehouse where I manufactured all the pieces that were part of my projects. I went on like this for some time, until there wasn´t enough room. What I did was to rent a much bigger one, which only had small modules. It had been an automobile garage and had a small construction and the rest consisted in a hole more than 2 meters deep. I remember that inside the hole, which was more than 2000 square meters, there were fruit trees such as avocado (or guacamoles, as others call them), nuts, figs, grapes, and so on and so forth. In fact, it had many varieties of fruit.

When I found this plot of land, I didn´t know that it was about to be auctioned by the Bank. When I leant about that I started to do the paperwork to be able to participate in the auction. I knew and was convinced that I couldn´t lose this land for a simple reason: when I had changed location, it took me two weeks to move all the machinery, tools and equipment I had acquired and which were fundamental to carry out my projects. The day of the auction arrived and there were only two people making offers, the Bank that had the mortgage on it and me who really needed to obtain the land. After a series of offers and counter offers and after 2 hours of negotiation, the judge awarded it to me. At that time I felt terribly happy and automatically started dreaming. I started building a big warehouse, offices; I bought machinery, equipment, tools and all the necessary things to have complete facilities which would be the foundation of my big dream.

In the meantime, my family and I went on living in that small flat and were still convinced that I could not incur any personal expense until I had everything for the efficient operation of the company.

Finally, the moment came when I could make a family investment. I started buying a plot of land, then I hired some architects and they started working on the future personal project which took 2 years to be built.

One the personal project was finished in 2006; I started to think again in my big industrial project.

I started to think HOW I could start with my industrial project. And I repeated something very similar to what I had done with the family project, the only thing that changed were the main characters. Firstly, I found a strategic piece of land with a good access to the main route that took us to the north and south of the country. After having found the land, I started working with the environmental permits and with architects and civil engineers to elaborate a project. One I had the plans and the project in paper; I started with the construction which took approximately 3 years. Why did it take so long? For a simple reason, I did it in different parts while I carried out the projects in a warehouse we had temporarily built with containers. As soon as we had finished the first half of the warehouse, we moved and went on with the construction plan.

Meanwhile, the other warehouse was used to carry out smaller projects; it had always been kept for very especial things. And now I am thinking HOW I organize the Academy Specialists which will be my contribution to many young people who do not have the means to obtain certifications.

This big industrial project was finished in 2010, and is a nice project as it has the possibility of being expanded in the future.

In previous chapters I have mentioned that I have had important failures and falls and due to this I changed the strategy and started to focus more on providing services at the clients´ premises. This is independent; we are still working on the industrial project.

Take this piece of advice as the experience life offers. Every time you face failure or a fall, change your strategy automatically. And do not think of failure or falls beforehand, because you will help them reach you. For this reason, work in the present and dream of the future. Only bear in mind your dreams start when you start to make some little changes that generate as a consequence of the things you do and which bring you closer and closer to your dreams.

Another piece of advice that has been particularly useful for me is that you shouldn´t talk about your dreams to people who do not vibrate in your same wavelength. I have also made this mistake. There will always be people who say "and why haven´t you told me that you were doing this or that?"

Do not let anybody spoil your dreams; carry them out first, so that envious people can only give you feedback. Take it as an opportunity for self growth.

Passion

You have to feel passion for what you do and this will make a big difference.

Passion is the fuel of our mind and heart. With passion it is easier to move forward. Passion is a fundamental element when setting up a new business. Without passion, we cannot move forward, without passion we get stagnant. Without passion it is impossible to get back on your feet after failure or a fall, which will inevitably happen some time or another. Remember that if you are committed with your business, but you do not act with passion, you are surely on the road to failure and fall. The courage to do everything you want to do in life will be determined by your actions, decisions and determinations.

If you cannot show or find this passion, or if you are paralyzed by internal fear, the answer is to focus on this objective you are pursuing in life. Like this, you will be able to abandon any internal fear you might have. If your real objective in life is what you are doing, you will have to deal with a series of obstacles and drawbacks; but if you are well focused, you won´t realize when you are weathering storms. If what you are doing bores you, then you are not connected to your purpose in life.

I have gone through passionate moments in my life as a businessman, and this was of great help for me to overcome falls and continue with my business without losing focus on my objective.

For example in 2015 a big project did not work properly and for the whole year we paid for the completion of the project until May 2016. This is clearly a company responsible for its commitments. I started feeling the consequences in the year 2016 when checks were rejected over and over again and the income flow was not enough to afford all our duties. We were technically broke.

I remember I was with my accounting and finance people at the office, planning and trying to find the HOW we could respond to our duties, and as if by magic the telephone stopped ringing. I told those who were present at that time that a client had already phoned me to ask for a requirement but that nobody answered. I immediately answered that I would ask the people at the department of proposals study and development to answer call him back. To my surprise, the telephone line had been cut. Imagine reaching the point at which your telephone service is cut. I felt devastated but I headed directly to my car and I drove to Santiago and I paid for the telephone bill. I did not want to tell anybody to do this for me because the company didn´t have in its account 2000 dollars to pay for the telephone bill in due time. Once I got to

Santiago, I walked to the place where I had to pay, but, again a test life had for me, the place was not the indicated one to pay because we had exceeded the extra term granted after expiration dates. I was not discouraged and went on walking to the offices where I could pay. I remember I had to make a queue for more than two hours. I thought, "These are tests" and I internally repeated this over and over again.

Once I was back to my office after having paid for the telephone bill, there was nobody. I went to my office, I sat down and spent some time thinking about what was there was in store for me and I told myself, "now I will gather courage and I promise this will be my graduation test, and I will use all my personal savings to save the company". In fact, this was my determination. There is a famous phrase from the book *Think and Become Rich* by Napoleón Hill that reads: "I will burn all my boats and I will be left with no choice at all, to live or die".

Somebody else might have said "and so well, come what may". We have to be in complete command of what we are doing and this commitment involves us personally, with all our body, dreams and money; we offer all our personal resources without thinking we could lose them all. This is determination, passion, internal strength and courage.

I don´t want you to experience failure, disappointment, falls or any other setback in life. I want you to connect with my experience and to use this connection to overcome any difficult or complex situation.

When there is passion, there is engagement. Passion is real commitment. You should feel passion at moments of trouble and of great achievement.

Passion is the inner fuel and energy that sets us in motion. If commitment is real as regards the objective, your whole body is full of passion.

Positive Thinking

Our thoughts have to be centered on what we desire

Imagining our dreams and desires does not set the path. It is positive thinking that transforms a problem into a challenge.

If you are enthusiastic about your business, and due to life circumstances, things are not going well, I can´t ask you not to be disappointed by setbacks, because sometimes you might not feel well. But if you are determined to challenge yourself, you need wisdom and peace of mind to think clearly how to overcome this lack of enthusiasm threatening your business.

In 2003, my business was already in operation and I had 100 employees. I did everything at that time; I even paid fortnight wages personally. Together with these payments I offered incentives to those who had reached our goals. As I paid them, I asked them if they were at ease with their contract and payment and they happily answered that it was more than good and I was very happy to see them happy. After finishing payments, everything was in its perfect place. However, after I had paid, I was left penniless, because duties come first.

The problems you may have in due time will turn into lessons and will make you stronger.

Posture

We always need to take an active and energetic posture.

Our posture is the way we express ourselves. A good posture increases our chances to succeed because it gives us objectivity.

Being objective implies honesty in our words and responsibility for our commitments. Being objective allows us to establish a deeper and more respectful communication.

We should also be aware of the importance of the voice. When we make a question, we can pay attention to the assertiveness and self-confidence of the person in front of us, but do not let this deceive us. Sometimes people pretend to undertake an obligation but in the end, they disregard it completely and make lots of excuses.

When we need information, it has to be congruent, legitimate and objective. We need to understand causes and reasons to undergo a change in our mindset and this will offer growth to our business solutions.

Resilience

Perseverance is the path to be followed not to be defeated by adverse situations that occur in life.
We react under pressure and we need to be full of energy and high spirits not to collapse when something complex happens in our life.

Resilience is the ability to overcome something that makes most of the people collapse and abandon their dreams.

It is important to be resilient because inevitably we will encounter many obstacles in life and will suffer numerous falls.

Obstacles are situations relatively easy to overcome but falls are more difficult. Many times when we fall, we might want to stand still and cry and we may think that the problem will be solved on its own some way or another and we do not look for solutions. We think everything is already lost.

But a thoroughbred businessman knows he has go stand up and keep on fighting, trying to find the best solutions. When you fall, you should think that what is happening to you at that moment is not the important thing but what you will see at the end of your journey. They are stages of the process, even if they can be tough.

In fact, resilience is what connects the end of something with its beginning, because even if you fall, you will stand up again, as there is an objective in your heart.

We should always be in control of our decisions and aware that our attitude will define our future.

Vision

*We should clearly see that every
business starts as a small one; but we
have to be convinced that we will turn it
into a bigger one.
Our vision allows us to imagine a
project finished before starting it.*

Dream of learning new techniques and the development of new methods; obtain certifications, create brands and patents for your ideas.

Stay away from difficult words. Exporting is the key to the growth of businessmen.

Manage assets at a long term. Methodologies can be patented.

Think of assets that can endure the passing of time. A good example of these models is the administration of assets and property. Then set up a company to manage its capital. Everybody knows that a good investment to prevent capital from disappearing would be to buy plots of land, but ... are they profitable? Sometimes they aren´t.

For land to be profitable, we should look after its maintenance, collect rent and commission. How is it possible to collect from

SUGGESTIONS FOR ENTREPRENEURS 163

both sides? One good example is seen in the case of McDonald's.

Be sustainable. Being sustainable means that your profitability lasts in time and that the community benefits as well.

Let´s help our community not to pollute and to look after the environment with our example. This means to be sustainable. It means to contribute to save electricity, to auto generate energy, for example. It is about giving fishing rods, not fish.

Why is it important to set a list of dreams? Because good energy generates good energy, it is that simple. Besides, when you write it with full awareness, and go to sleep thinking about your dreams, you may wake up with different ideas. This is very simple, the mind develops your ideas unconsciously while you sleep, work or do whatever you have to do, it´s that simple.

And in order to win, in whichever realm, good energy is a must. What is good energy? Good predisposition comes from dreaming projects that are beneficial to our companies and to our families.

When you set on the journey of thinking how you can fulfill your dream, always do it consciously and write it down immediately. Start thinking this dream for an hour and do it for 3 days. What will happen is that it will be stored in your mind unconsciously and as a result of this, your brain will send you signs of where it can spot opportunities to make them come true. Pay attention to these signs, because sometimes people say "I have a recurrent idea". This is how your mind starts working when you do these exercises. I assure you that if you do them with faith and perseverance, you will see the results. And don´t be afraid of criticism, be afraid of your lack of enthusiasm, because this does reduce your energy.

Clients

Undoubtedly, the client is the main focus of attention in any company that provides products and services, because all the marketing plans and strategies must be focused, developed and implemented according to the clients´ needs.

Empathy

Find the way to empathize with your clients

Empathy entails to understanding what the other knows, feels and needs.

It is necessary to demonstrate that you, with your empathy will make your client catch your way of being. This closes deals, because you offer reliability to your client. We have to study closely the clients´ needs and find the way to help them. If you achieve this you will gain a faithful client, loyal to your products or services.

Big businesses closed because somebody is able to satisfy the needs and requirements of clients.

If you are willing to find a position in the market, be different from your competitor. Try to find a way to give added value to your products or services. Be obsessive as regards your client; show him that you can deliver a product or service before the agreed time.

Make people working for you think like you, act like you, have a real obsession for the client.

When we describe how we have to behave on a daily basis, the first thing I emphasize is that empathy is the fundamental basis for good communication with people and that it opens up a whole world of opportunities which can only be seized being empathic.

If you are an empathic person, you can change the life and destiny of a person, with only small things such as a smile, a good morning, good afternoon, good evening, nice to see you, I would like you to feel very well or I thank your empathy. Clearly, these are the messages we should transmit constantly so that the day could be a door open to a world of infinite possibilities that can only be seen through empathy.

Remember that the world we live in needs people with values; this requires our contribution to these people that need support. Sometimes, with a little help, you get a smile in return and what is more, you can empathize with your neighbor.

Heart

It is fundamental that if you are going to give your coworkers a chance, you do it from your heart.

In life we have many options, as businessmen, to offer our collaborators the opportunity to grow as people and as professionals. Generally, this generates a higher commitment on the part of collaborators due to a simple reason, they can see that what you are doing will directly benefit them as well.

Many books deal with the need of separating and setting our feeling aside when evaluating corporate matters.

I completely disagree. It is precisely our heart and the love we have for our mission, not only as entrepreneurs but also as owners and individuals responsible for our dreams, that make us put our heart in our tasks and objectives.

In times of growth, volatility and conflicting views (even sometimes impossible to compromise), my experience confirms my belief of putting our heart in control. It is from there that our major commitment will become evident and our strongest will and most creative acts will arise.

Trust

Only with courage can we grow. And growing requires the maximum courage.

Once, a client required some advice from me. He asked me if I could help him see a way to find a change for a project that was not going well. It had been assigned to a company in the same field and they were unable to find a solution to revert the results.

I remember that we spoke on the phone for an hour; I asked him some questions and suggested he had to allocate human resources to the project. I also mentioned they should provide them with more equipment and tools. The client asked me "with the quantity you are proposing, can we solve this in 10 days?" I answered "In fact, you can but you have to work day and night shifts".

We can say then that trust saves time, because we don´t have to "double check that what somebody is saying is true, or go on looking for other alternatives. Instead, when we really trust others, we know that what they are saying is the truth.

Then, we can say that trust is built with little things which are turned into facts. When do people start trusting you? When you demonstrate your value through experience.

Value

We have to take care of our clients and find a way of generating added value to the products and services we are delivering.

Our clients should not receive only words. The value we offer through our acts in products and services is what helps them grow.

When we are carrying out an activity, it is necessary to understand clearly that our clients will always require more. However, it is important to consider that when the client needs more of our services, it means that we have to assign real importance to the things we are doing and also find the way to be different from our competitors.

For this reason, you should always be on the alert to see what your client needs, ask which his needs are, ask him personally which extra service can add value to his operation to demonstrate that your interest is real and genuine, which benefits you have to make his activities more profitable and quicker without damaging the cost of the service. Be constantly thinking of innovation.

Innovation is always appreciated by clients because they know that to be competitive, they depend on the improvements they apply to their products and services, or on the creation of new products and services.

Nowadays, to be a competent and competitive supplier, you should be capable of offering something different. When I say something different, I mean that we have to take the initiative, as far as our products and services are concerned, and be ready to approach our clients and have a talk at the right time so that company leaders can understand what we are offering.

Remember that when we refer to added value, we can offer it in everything we do. Added value is not only limited to the fact that we can deliver good service or a product, it means much more than a good performance in all our activities. Added value is the difference the client has not even considered. So this added value proves to be a surprise additional to what we are delivering.

Collaborators

They are the people who support you to carry out a task, a project, or a service and who are willing to commit themselves to ensure that everything that has been planned will be completed as has been previously agreed.

Communications

We should always tell our coworkers that communication is the key to achieve good results

Communication is essential so that everybody has the same expectations. We have to consider that communications must be constant with the people engaged in the development process of your company products or services.

Surely, in communications we will find the biggest revolution: the way to communicate with people has changed since the inclusion of the cell phone, Whatsapp and all the new technologies of present and the future.

The correct use of language is a critical factor of success in communications. They must be clear and honest in critical situations and must help understand what is going on without losing trust.

The absence of good communications makes people have their own interpretation of the facts. If we are not able to help them clarify their points of view, we will never have one unique official voice.

It should be verified if the message that reached our collaborators is the one that wanted to be transmitted. You will be surprised to know that many times when you check what the other person understood, it is not what you intended to say. When you want to address other people, it is fundamental they understand the same for the sake of a clear point of view.

Empowerment

You should be always empowering your coworkers so that they feel important and help you reverse results without exerting pressure on them.

Thanking people and telling them how important they are for your company is fundamental to make people feel committed and grateful. This generates in them an inner energy that drives them towards the achievement of results.

Empowerment always generates results such as meeting the deadline of a technical and economic offer, shorter execution times, and favorable economic results and so on. Empowering people makes them carry out their activities without causing inconveniences.

Disregarding the support your people are offering definitely makes them work without enthusiasm or the desire to comply with their tasks and undertakings. They feel they are not taken into consideration, and in general this is translated into bad results for the company and its founder.

We have to understand that thanking and showing how much you appreciate the people who are at your side cooperating to make your dream come true generates empowerment on their part.

Active Listening

If you want to obtain the recognition of your coworkers start by listening to them so that you can offer congruent answers

Active listening in the business world is a valuable and important asset. Listening to your coworkers is highly enriching, as well as listening to our clients, suppliers, partners and contractors.

Listening generates the feedback necessary to obtain the information we would not access otherwise.

For example, if you listen to your suppliers with attention, they can offer you something that can help you improve your processes, the quality of your products or services, improve your pricing, lower your costs, increase the useful life of your products, shorten execution times or even help introduce a new service you couldn´t offer before, contributing to the diversification of your proposal while helping your clients with their problems and needs.

Get people involved

It is always important to ask for their opinion and get workers involved in the business. They will help you because they will feel part of the solution.

Being part of a team does not mean to have followers but people cooperating.

Getting people involved by asking them to give you their opinion, an idea, advice or a different approach, will give them a more important role. A simple example is when we gather our people to obtain from them an improvement and we ask them directly HOW they could improve a situation. They will immediately give you their point of view, and the result you will get will be that you have to change your strategy. Furthermore, you made your improvement project stronger because you were capable of listening to your collaborators´ opinions.

All the important achievements I had in life have been the result of the engagement of all the people who had participated with their opinion and with significant effort to make a project work.

The approach you give to your decisions must be integrating your people in order to obtain a richer point of view.

Growth

Many times we consider growing, and the first thing that comes to our mind is that growth must be economic. However, there is a completely logic reason, which is the following: first grow in mind and soul, and as a consequence your finances will also grow.

Economic and financial issues

The newest model of a machine with a broken engine is more likely to prevent you from carrying out the project, than an old machine with an impeccable engine.

I use this example as an analogy with the company. The car, the newest model of the machine is the economic structure and the engine is the financial structure.

The economy of a company is represented by results, making profits or losses, that´s to say the business results, by doing our job efficiently or inefficiently and by who we offer our services to. Sales or the lack of sales have to do with the economy of the company, as well as producing goods or services, buying and selling machinery, inputs, power and raw materials, etc.

The finances of a company have to do with what the company needs to operate. No matter which size, activity, geographical location or number of partners they may have, companies need certain elements to operate.

To have these elements, it is necessary to obtain resources; that is money or financing.

SUGGESTIONS FOR ENTREPRENEURS

This money can be our own (the company´s or the partners´ money) or may come from third parties (banks, suppliers, the State).

The financial structure of a company has two parts: investment and financing sources.

Both are equally important to allow the business to operate and grow. And both require a lot of knowledge and permanent attention for the correct execution of projects.

The financial equilibrium of a company needs to be coherent and balanced as regards what is invested and the financial sources used. The more mature a company is and the more expanding plans it has, the greater the need of resources and financing will be.

Export

Exporting is growing and this growth is necessary when the local market is saturated or when there is an increasing demand of our product or service abroad.

When we start a company, we first set it up, then it grows and finally the alternative to go on growing is to export. My recommendation here is that when you want to export your company, the first and most important thing is to create a synergy with a team really committed to the objective of going abroad. If not, a lot of inconveniences arise and you won´t achieve your objective.

One example in my own experience would be when we wanted to export our services. We did it in Peru; it took us 2 years and we lost a lot of money.

Firstly, it is fundamental to understand that during certain periods of time, we won´t make any profit, but only invest. So at the beginning, there must be some reserves to allocate to this objective with a clear understanding of the return of this investment, both as regards time and money. You might experience two years of losses, which can be avoided if things are done properly. It is the same as planting and

SUGGESTIONS FOR ENTREPRENEURS 183

harvesting, which would be the return on this investment. It might not happen the following year, nor the other or the next one. It is fundamental to know this and have a professional planning and the proper financial structure to support this.

We must invest with commitment.

The most important thing at the time of exporting is to emphasize the fact that we must have people who share our same vision and the same enthusiasm to carry out the project successfully. If the desire is not the same, the same levels of commitment are never met. In this situation, in spite of the fact that the entrepreneur could be highly enthusiastic, if his team did not accompany him, even if he offered the resources, the company would not work.

There are two ways of exporting. One is to form your own team and the other is to find partners outside. But my advice is that if there is a person within your circle, it is advisable that he starts negotiations abroad and he himself chooses other people to accompany him, the location, the resources, suppliers, clients, etc.

Assets

The company's assets are divided into tangible and intangible assets. Both constitute the value of the company.

The company's tangible assets are those which can be easily quantified and which appear in balance sheets. Those include land, machinery, buildings, vehicles, etc. They can be seen and touched. All of them are necessary for the correct operation of the company. If you did not have your own tangible assets, you could rent them.

Intangible assets are those which cannot be seen or touched. These include, for example, know-how, the name or brand, a good name and reputation, etc. Not all of them do have a value. Only those that allow the company to make a positive difference as regards the products or services offered will have a value.

The willingness of a client to pay extra for a service or a product is the evidence of the positive value of our intangible assets.

Indirect Growth

Our growth will indirectly help many people.

Do not just notice the benefits of an action. Growing indirectly brings about a lot of spiritual, physical and economic growth.

Use your leisure time productively.

Many people commute for more than 45 minutes both in the morning and in the afternoon. This represents 180 minutes a day and 360 hours a year; almost two working months per year. We may listen to audio books on our telephones; from novels to disconnect for a while, to books of management, languages or interviews. There are audio books, talks and videos on whatever might interest you. There are thousands of audios that can help us in our project.

The key is how you want to live your life, for this same reason I gave a very simple example of how you can make the most of your time and feed your brain with important information that will allow you to grow on a permanent basis.

Challenges

It simply means to look for new ways that will allow you to be a determined person in life.

Attitude

We have to understand that only a few of us do not need to go through obstacles or crises in life to achieve success. However, most of us have to overcome drawbacks and crises to achieve success.

When there are challenges, it is extremely important to talk to people with a positive, assertive and determined attitude as regards our acts and words.

For example, it is very important to inform people the degree of difficulty of jobs. The projects in our field require a lot of discipline and commitment and we will find plenty of obstacles that may be quite uncomfortable. That is why it is very important for each participant of a team to have such commitment to his peers as to generate in them the attitude of being convinced that they will make it. This attitude will ensure the possibility of reaching the results desired.

Tell yourself that attitude is fundamental each time you carry out an activity, even a minor one, be convinced that your attitude will make it come true. Attitude represents us and our situations.

With the right attitude and by means of visualizations that will take us through time, we will see how our life will be, how we will be, how the people at our side will be and also how people you will help one day will be.

I remember a time when I was very stressed out because things were not working well. I was seeing how the company was collapsing and I couldn´t support it because the economy of the country was a disaster. We didn´t have enough contracts to afford the payroll and to make things worse, basic and operative costs were going up. At that time, I was feeling down, my body ached and without noticing it, I was round-shouldered and with a pain in my chest. I remember that I went to the car, I filled the tank and I drove aimlessly without listening to anything, I even turned off the mobile phone and I drove many kilometers. When I was hungry I stopped at a restaurant to have something to eat and I sat down. I was deeply immersed in thought. I asked myself "why should I be like this if my life is not that bad? If there are people who are really suffering in this life? And the problem I have is part of the growth of my business. I realized I had to take this as a blessing and look for a way out."

As advice, in times like this, it is important to take some time to think things over and do the necessary changes. You have to understand that you cannot indulge in letting yourself feel down.

Life is so beautiful that we cannot even waste a minute of it. That was why that word, ATTITUDE was fundamental to me. It came to my life when I was a little boy, my mother always told me "son, to become someone in life you need to have the right attitude.

You can obtain what you want in life and you will never get a NO for an answer if you have the right attitude"; and you were right mother; you had always been right.

Learn

You have to learn from the problems you face

There will always be problems. It is very important to try to avoid them by means of planning and action. But on some occasions, due to unforeseeable situations, sudden changes or unpredictable events, problems occur one after the other.

My experience taught me to see each problem as a new opportunity. An opportunity to grow and learn using the information obtained at these situations.

I learnt something different from each problem I had and I treasured each of these lessons to prevent similar situations and be able to offer advice before this unpredictable problems take place.

We have to take into account that sometimes problems occur because we relax and neglect our duties and leave things for the very last minute. Look for a way to solve your problems right now. My experience shows me that some of the advice given by books and audio books is very congruent.

Anticipate

If you are confident that everything you are doing is going all right, it is always important to consider what could happen if things changed.

I remember that in 2011 we had lots of contracts and within them there was a very special one that required 300 permanent people to carry out maintenance tasks in a copper flotation plant where we were working from Monday to Friday.

For no special reason, we used to park the vans allocated to that project in our industrial premises. All of a sudden a very kind neighbor had a talk with one of the workers in charge of transport and offered his premises to park these vans. The transport chief thought it was a good idea because our neighbor was at less than 30 meters of our headquarters.

On Monday, when these vans had to leave at 6:00 AM to the construction site, we found out that the fuel of the 12 vans we had left there had been stolen. There wasn´t even enough fuel to reach the petrol station to fill in the tank and head for the construction site.

It took us more than 2 hours to solve the problem. Our client was angry due to our delay. The biggest inconvenience in this situation wasn´t the loss of fuel, but the fact that our leaders arrived late. The client already had the 300 people but they couldn´t do anything, because a client cannot give orders directly to the workers of collaborating companies.

The most complex situation was that all the clients have obligations and their times are not flexible. Due to our delay, they had to postpone the departure of those teams; and that meant that they had to account for this situation to all the managers, the managers to the directors and it supposed a tough reprimand for us, because the client does not understand any reason when critical teams are involved in the operation.

I hope that this experience encourages you to verify each detail of your business. And if your business is very big, you have to insist your collaborators to verify all the details. Tell them not to trust those who pretend to act in goodwill. The only thing we got when we trusted our neighbor was losing our client´s credibility and our trust in a person.

For this reason, we need to be more cautious and start to check and double check all the processes and potential problems that might arise in the course of our projects on a regular basis.

Look for a way out

If you are in a complicated situation, you need to be in a position that allows you to find the way out of it.

Critical moments require the search of creative solutions. Creativity, flexibility and positive thinking are the key, as well as the participation of coworkers and specialists.

To be able to find the effective way out, the company has to take a close look at itself with a sharp view that favors understanding, as regards any possible aptitude available, and ask itself which solutions can be generated to produce a deep change in the drawbacks the company is experiencing.

Each person in each area has a different experience, capabilities and perspectives of the problem, as each of them sees it and lives it in accordance with the impact it causes to their sector and area of responsibility. This includes suppliers and clients.

It is not only necessary to look at the inside but also at the outside because problems can generate other problems if they are not solved with the integral view of all the parties involved.

Focus on solutions

You can´t focus on problems, you should focus on solutions.

In my experience, focusing on problems is completely absurd. Focusing on the fact that everything went wrong, on who was to blame, on how much loss it caused, etc., does not let us concentrate on solutions.

The importance of focusing on solutions implies finding the quickest way to solve most of the situations.

On many occasions, when we focus on the problem we end up finding more problems. But when we focus on solutions we will find solutions.

For example, if the budget to manufacture a special piece was wrong and we focus on finding the causes or the origin of the mistake, we will find that it wasn´t properly evaluated, that the planning was not good, that the time estimate was not accurate, etc.

Now, let´s see how we can reverse this situation. We have a wrongly prepared budget. Firstly let´s check if execution times are comfortable, secondly evaluate if we can translate the daily cost of workers to a value for the result of the finished project, thirdly, let´s evaluate all the alternatives we have to obtain better prices for the purchase of materials. Finally, let´s analyze if all the costs were covered after having finished all the analyses.

My recommendation is sending a letter to the client to inform him that we have made a mistake in the estimate and that this will directly affect the company and indirectly the workers; and that the situation entails impairment in the execution of the project, both for the workers and the company.

After this brief letter we have to wait for an answer. If the client is sensible, he will call you to review the estimate. If he doesn´t want to get involved, he will tell you that this is your problem, that he had also asked other companies for different estimates and that you had been granted the execution of the project.

For this reason I insist that first you have to take some time, check thoroughly all the factors that influence any type of estimate for a task or project, plan in detail all the activities, go over all the estimates for the purchase of materials and verify if you can generate deals from the result of the tasks with your collaborators. The result of all the revisions will prevent you from making mistakes, which can be very painful if you assume them, mainly if your business is just taking off. And never forget that as you are growing, the level of mistakes is gradually more painful.

How to achieve dreams?

You will always be able to achieve anything. You only have to think how.

I have said on many occasions that asking oneself how? is fundamental to start a business; and it is so much so that I say it again. When in the face of a challenge, a problem or a new situation I wonder how to deal with it, I share my strategy. This has always given me the best results and I still use it and teach it to all my coworkers and even use it in our team meetings.

Firstly, I prepare a list of the problems, new projects and challenges and I complete this list with the possible number of solutions I can think of. I include absolutely all of them, I don´t evaluate them at this stage. I just let my brain flow and I go over the different alternatives.

For example, if I wonder: how can I do X? Then I elaborate a list of 30 possible answers. I choose the 3 which I objectively consider most likely to be feasible and I dismiss the other 27. From these 3 answers, I elaborate 3 answers more for each answer, more detailed, sharper and more specific. Then I will have the 3 initial answers plus the 9 additional ones. This amounts to 12 answers, which are more detailed, sharper and more accurate. Only then do I start analyzing. I wonder what would happen if I did this, what would happen if I didn´t do this and I go on doing the same thing with each of the 12 solutions I have thought of. It is there that I have all the information I need to arrive at the best solution or feasible path and then take the best decision.

Details

It is essential to remember that we have to go over every process and state of affairs if we wish to perform things successfully.

It is very important for us to do things in the best possible way. It is very important to trust your instincts, but your instincts have to be well aligned and trained and defined because life is made of many small situations.

When a project is started, we should take into account very important aspects, such as strategies, objectives, tactics and we have to be highly trained in aptitudes such as anticipation, revision, vision, etc.

It is like dancing, like a jigsaw made of tiny parts that make a big difference in your life if you want to be an entrepreneur who provides a good service or product.

It is essential to do things the best you can; not only important things, but also small things.

These small things, "fine" things are nothing but details and details really make a big difference in what you plan to do.

Remember that when we start a business or make our business grow, it can only resist the passing of time if details are taken care of.

Details are fundamental pieces to keep a company growing and are also the flame that keeps love alive, the key to make a client feel satisfied, to live in harmony with your mates, to keep good relationships at work and to relate with everything you want to relate with. Everything is related to a single word: details. All this is contained in a single word: details.

Detail is the magic word of big things, by means of details we can dream of the smallest things that give life to great things.

Experience

You have to keep on training and preparing yourself so that your business or businesses grow with your experience

Experience is one of the key tools to achieve business objectives. The curve of facts and consequences of the past evokes courses of action to follow which will result in more success and less failure.

To make good use of your experience and not to be confused in processes, it is fundamental to analyze completely and from different angles and perspectives the facts and actions of the past, that´s to say what the company experienced in the last years.

But experience may sometimes get anchored when the market is complicated. Seize the opportunity life offers you, moreover when you are well acquainted with the subject you are dealing with. The surroundings or circumstances are highly changeable.

I suggest that when you do not possess the required experience, you look for people who have it. Make an economic deal with them which is beneficial for both of you. This will help you not to make many mistakes that can cost you a lot of money.

Constant Improvement

Bear in mind that you have to pursue the continuous improvement of what you do.

Continuous improvement is a process enrooted in the soul of every successful company. In the world of corporations it is widely admitted that it constitutes one of the vital and most valuable processes for any company since it is what allows it to endure the passing of time.

In the face of a highly changing, volatile, uncertain and fast paced world, the only way to adjust is by means of a continuous improvement of all the operations and processes of an organization.

Improving supposes growing and adjusting. Not growing implies losing and dying at some time.

The concepts of change in this new era force us to be more creative and to look for ways and alternatives, to be able to break schemes and be efficient and effective. However, the interest to take care of people is at the base of all new changes. Besides, we must also be concerned with the protection of the environment.

Opportunities

You have to be aware of the fact that when you start your own business and want to become independent, you will find a considerable number of obstacles ... the most important thing is to know this will happen. And once you have overcome them new doors will open with plenty of new opportunities.

As soon as you start a project the level of complexity starts increasing. Many times unexpected obstacles get in your way and new difficulties appear in different areas and you have to solve them successfully.

This implies the sophisticated exercise of understanding, flexibility, creativity and effective problem solving, together with the right and timely decision making.

Are all of us prepared for this? The truth is that we are not. In most of the cases, those in charge do not possess the persistence, resilience or confidence required to overcome a process of continuous and mounting difficulties. It is there where the difference between succeeding or failing lies.

Strategy

It is not difficult to lift a 10-ton-load if you have the suitable equipment.

Strategy

When you feel things are not going all right, change your strategy

Strategy is the map or compass that indicates where the company or organization must head for.

A good strategy may be the key to success. Its design is based on the correct interpretation of the reality of the organization both as regards its present and future.

To be successful, every organization must have a strategy to review; double check and re define on a permanent basis.

Why? Because designing a good strategy is fundamental to set the path and define the destiny of the company.

Which resources are needed to achieve this? All the resources we have at present and the ones we will need tomorrow to achieve our goals.

Strategy is closely related with the company´s objectives and tactics, very often being confused.

To understand the difference:

An example of strategy could be growing in the long term and being the leader in the market of a country, while an objective could be to achieve the different goals that will make the strategy to be applied successfully.

To this end, tactics are used, which are described as the group of acts towards the fulfillment of objectives that will lead us to meet the general strategy.

An example would be if the company in question has the strategy of being a leader in certain field of industry in its country, being its objectives to draw an X percentage of the market from each competitor and the tactics would be to advertise at massive or digital events, social networks, etc. In general, this applies to all the companies whose business is related to products and services.

In general, we use techniques and strategies to carry out any activity related to our field. For example: to recruit, we have a database and besides, we require people to platforms of employment search and then we hire them to carry out a big or specific task. This is carried out before the execution: we perform safe working procedures, histograms, S curves, Gant Chart, working methodology, etc. All these are part of the strategy of a services company.

Strategies change according to the type of business. Even artists have their own strategy, which is in general to rehearse and try to introduce changes to their routines, create new things for the public to see and feel that this artist is making changes constantly. And this, will undoubtedly, be the key to success in the profession.

Anchors – Important

If you need to gather more courage to deal with difficult situations, make an analogy of how your past was and use this past as an anchor not to move backwards in life.

When an entrepreneur states that in the face of a challenge he has to analyze the anchors of his past, he refers to finding situations full of happiness and bringing them back to his life. And with this happy moment find the energy to achieve success.

So, if I am complicated for any personal reason or circumstance or I am being challenged by a project, it is obviously important to search in my personal history what can be really useful to anchor my best moments and, represent them to improve those I am facing. It is very important to feel associated to the best moments.

It is known that knowledge is acquired in an associative way. This means that to learn or develop a new scheme or a new course of action, we need to manage or compare this new action we are about to follow with something of the past that inspires us to go beyond.

Change of Paradigm

You should look for a way of turning your expenditure into benefits.

One of the true challenges of businessmen is to understand the costs of a project or operation.

In general, businessmen consider them sunk costs or money expenditure without anything in return.

Real businessmen try to make expenditure produce a secondary effect. They transform every expense, every cost into real investment.

For example: many organizations consider training an expense, but it is in fact an investment cost, simply because you will count with trained people and obtain better results. That means that this is a win situation for the person who received training and a win situation for the company that achieved better results with this training.

Another example would be to purchase state of the art machinery. This speeds processes, simplifies tasks and saves time. So, it is not a cost but an investment with higher benefits.

Every time you are going to invest, do not worry about the value, think of the benefits this will bring about.

Perseverance and Trust.

The battle has to be constant to generate the desired results. Perseverance generates trust.

To generate improvements there must be confidence and knowledge; not only theoretical, but practical knowledge as well. Clients must look for solutions and this generates trust. It is not enough to perceive that the supplier can sell us the solution; we have to feel sure that we will be able to implement it and make it work.

Trust is generated by making questions, such as:

—How would you suggest I start?

—Which are the advantages and disadvantages of the terms and resources that will be undertaken?

—Which are in general the critical factors of the product or service?

Success can be perceived when the client and the supplier understand the business and the needs. We all know that sometimes the cheapest alternative forces us to buy the solution twice and we also know that sometimes the most expensive thing is not necessarily the best.

The client and the supplier together should determine the path.

Make Contributions

If someone asks for your help, please give it to him without expecting anything in return.

The business activity generates a lot of benefits and contributions not only for the company itself. Its workers, suppliers, clients and the community where it is located are also direct or indirect beneficiaries of its activities in society.

As a businessman, you are an important factor in the creation of employment, in the training and learning of your employees, in the provision of products and services necessary for consumers or clients, in the purchase of the input used in your company, in the payment of tax and in every other contribution derived from your company in the benefit of society.

Contributing to the development of neighboring communities, also produce effects in society.

Not only do we have to think in direct or indirect assistance that is generated through a country or community. We have to think as well, how we can change the vision of some entrepreneurs who can be out of breath, due to the lack of the appropriate guidance of an entrepreneur who had gone through the same experiences. This book is a contribution to the development and personal growth of people.

Limiting Beliefs

If your beliefs originate obstacles in your growth, analyze if you are in the right business.

If your belief is that forests are vital for the maintenance of the ecosystem and the generation of the air we breathe, you shouldn´t be in the wooden furniture business.

Your beliefs should be aligned with your organizational objectives and the general strategy of the business. It is obvious to say that you should believe in what you do and that what you do must be aligned to your dream. This will make the performance of your activities smoother and more enjoyable and with the best chances of fulfilling your goals.

Sometimes we believe that we are in the right business and we do not realize that failures outnumber successes. It is then that we have to analyze ourselves and think over if we have the desire and the energy to make it work. We have been convinced for long that we have to pay a price to be somebody in life. It is also important that you start thinking about other businesses that may change the life you are leading now.

There are some businesses that can change your income radically. We always have opportunities, but we have to look for them.

Always remember that our beliefs of being able to do business or the way we live our lives can always be changed.

Changes take place when we are convinced we can experience them. You only have to think constantly about the change you want for your life and how you will implement this change. You have to be fully convinced and this is only possible with positive thinking and constantly imagining the life you want to live and change. And this will be a huge move in your life: to change your personal history and consequently achieve a change in your beliefs that will take you to the level that you want to reach.

Diversification

It is always important to diversify and not to think that your client will be there for ever

Business diversification is one of the growing strategies a company has to implement. This is so basically because clients are constantly looking for alternatives that are more competitive and they always think that somebody else may treat them better.

Moreover, we have to diversify products or services. With this strategy you will increase your presence in the markets you are operating now and you will increase the trust your clients have in your brand.

If your company is diversified, make sure you do it very well, because your clients will value you according to how you focus on it.

Risks associated to a single client are highly dangerous; make sure you have the biggest amount of clients you can, diversifying all your products or services.

We should bear in mind that we have cycles and trends and that they may be quite difficult or complex. This doesn´t mean that you have to be constantly worried, this is just a tip I can give you. Because sometimes we think we are going up and nobody will stop us, and all of a sudden we have economic setbacks which can cost a lot of money.

Why do we need to diversify our business?

Among the most important factors that can lead to the decision of diversifying we can mention the following:

- A very concrete and specific scenario that depends on the basic competitive forces and on the structural characteristics of the industry.
- The general context where the company operates, such as social, political, technological, legal or economic pressure.
- The characteristics of the company that intends to move in this direction.

5 reasons to diversify a business

We should also take into account the following situations or needs:

1. Market Saturation

In very competitive markets and in some industrial sectors there is a strong oversaturation, because there are many companies offering the same services and products. Thanks to diversification new products and services can be offered in the markets.

2. Reducing risks

When we diversify clients and the services we offer, we minimize risks in the long run. Even if any of the activities fail, not all of them will. When we enlarge the income sources we reduce financial failure.

The failure of many projects with different clients is always more unlikely that failure in one single project.

3. Generating synergy

The development of new activities and the relationship with other clients is more important than what can be considered at first sight. The result will be the better performance of the group and the bigger control on the business.

4. Taking advantage of resources

Each company decides where to invest its extra resources and capacity to satisfy new clients and/or create a new product, service or relationships with new companies.

5. Investment Opportunities

It is interesting to invest in activities that may bring about profitability and growth possibilities.

Business diversification has many benefits, such as enlarging your target market, launching your product or service into new markets, improving your brand image, generating bigger income and better and deeper differences with competitors. Each company has to decide how to do this considering its own philosophy and objectives. Standing still and refusing to grow is never a good choice.

It is really important that everything you are doing, you do it with love, passion and a lot of energy.

Flexibility and Planning

Strategic planning supposes the search for the best alternatives and the introduction of a second strategy to change the original plan. Make sure you elaborate plans and strategies that will allow you to get away from any situation.

It is advisable to have a set of alternative plans that contemplate the different circumstances and possible changes in the face of a determined activity or objective.

WHY? Because markets change, clients change, circumstances change, governments change and markets also change. When the original plan loses its relevance or is likely to fail, the moment comes to analyze and evaluate the alternative plans mentioned before.

Alternative plans contemplate different combinations of tactics, actions and human, economic or other resources. In other words, they are commonly called Plan A, B, C, D, E.

Innovation

You have to innovate on a constant basis. Strategic innovation is the raw material of the future.

At present, companies are facing increasingly changing surroundings continuously evolving and gaining competitiveness. This is the reason why the key to success for all these companies that resist the passing of time in spite of the market situations is innovation.

Likewise, companies increasingly need to possess new dynamic strategies that will allow them to combine their resources and energies so that they can be at the service of continuous innovation. In this business context strategic innovation is fundamental.

In companies, strategic innovation is defined as the need to manage change with a look into the future with the objective of being more competitive and grow. As a result of this, new business management methods have come into scene, as well as a big range of instruments the objective of which is to manage innovation strategically.

Consequently, we can see that strategic innovation is about considering innovation as a business process that needs to be managed from a strategic perspective, so that the company obtains competitive advantages as it creates value for its clients and the company itself.

Achievements

The journey of entrepreneurship does not end in a year. You need more time to make it succeed without forgetting you can achieve it before that time too. Your attitude and perseverance will dictate the time to succeed.

After my long experience as an entrepreneur, I can state that to be a successful entrepreneur we must desire it deeply from our heart, from our DNA.

What happens in our lives is not important, real entrepreneurs will do what it takes to go on growing, building, creating, finding solutions, innovating and trying to find the way to improve things; in other words, to achieve their dreams.

Such is the spirit of a businessman, to pursue action and movement, which is the fundamental and irreplaceable basis.

An IDEA without ACTION is just a thought. An ACTION without an IDEA is a waste of time, but an IDEA in ACTION is what changes the world.

Managing your achievement in the correct way is the basis of your growth. Always remember that our improvement must be constant.

Measure

It is fundamental to be able to measure everything we do.

The marks projects left on me have taught me that you have to be constantly going over and measuring improvements. You cannot take for granted that everything is all right. Yes, afterwards, what a surprise! Different excuses appear, and excuses such as: "I thought the field engineer was good because the manager had recommended him, because another friend engineer had recommended him" and it´s always the same story. We have to be sure for once and for all that all the tools used in engineering are synchronized with the real facts on the working site.

Merits base on evaluating results. This is the way to prevent delays in projects and encourage productivity.

Besides, spread sheets allow you to check and double check constantly, together with all the Office tools and with more specific ones which can be acquired.

If a client has problems with times, this has to be measured. The important thing is to ask: where is specifically the delay? Did all the activities fall behind? Or just those that required the use of a machine that was not working properly? Was it necessary to complain to the workers who used this machine, when in fact nobody had measured the capacity of the tools?

A new business has to measure the level of satisfaction of their workers in relation with the projects carried out.

Satisfaction does not only generate in the activities we carry out but also in analyzing if the client recommends the service to others. I call this **value**.

The real measurement and meritocracy of a new business is not only determined by the quantity of clients it has but by being hired again or recommended to their clients and suppliers.

It is not enough to observe only clients; we also have to pay attention to communities, industries and regions. This is the view I encourage in entrepreneurs, observing their complete surroundings.

In sports the best example of meritocracy takes place. Both in team or individual sports, many people work for the trophy. Those who score more, keep a sustained performance in time and improve continuously are the ones at the top of rankings. The rest are mere intentions.

A very important anecdote in my life: I remember that for many years we hadn´t done maintenance works in a boiler. The truth is that very frequently clients trust the companies they hire so much that it is practically impossible to enter as a new supplier. Until one day, a company did not satisfy the client´s expectations and we had the great chance of carrying out maintenance tasks.

To do this, we created a procedure that was very well written, step by step. More than 250 people were going to participate in a direct way plus indirect people, amounting to a 30% more of the total staff for this contract.

But an unexpected obstacle appeared. We had a chief land engineer who had worked for us for many years and recommended another land engineer to perform the repairs in a specific part of the boiler. This engineer had already been recognized by the engineer in charge of the maintenance works who was also the manager of the contract.

The whole procedure was explained to him. Once the maintenance tasks had started, this land engineer gathered his staff, who was always with him, and started working.

When we started to carry out the complete repair works and days went by, our management required to consolidate all the information in accordance with the advances we were supposed to have made. We had been there for 3 days, when we noticed that the advance in the area corresponding to this land chief was completely wrong (this wasn´t bad, it was too bad!)

I required an investigation to analyze the cause of such a deviation and I was informed that the chief had not carried out the procedure as had been originally planned.

What happened finally? What happened was that we had failed to do a real and constant follow-up to this part of the maintenance from the first day. That's to say that **we didn't measure every point of the work,** we didn't supervise and the result was quite unfavorable.

I remember that I went to the place where this maintenance was being carried out every day. I checked that I had visited every point, but I hadn't visited precisely that point of work because we trusted that land chief too much. I was always insisting on checking everything but I relaxed and trusted and never checked that point of work.

Unfortunately, we had a significant delay that only we could detect. I asked: which was the reason for the change of strategy and why was it so bad? The first thing I did was to leave the point of work to think things clearly and let my mind think for a while before addressing the engineer in charge who also was the manager of the contract. I asked to be given an action plan to make up for that delay deviation. I needed the information that same afternoon, at 4 PM Chilean hour maximum.

The idea was that it had to be at that time to give us time to react. And if the client noticed that deviation, the idea was to explain it. We would also tell them that we had to reinforce that point of work with more staff. Afterwards we had to meet the client in 3 hours. I asked to be called to be informed briefly about the situation. I needed a more detailed action plan to reverse that result. When I called, he told me the following: this land engineer had not followed the instructions as he should have and, he carried out the job as he had always done in other boilers. I asked him to have a conversation with this man and to tell him that what he was doing was generating negative results and that we had to get back to the original strategy.

They had a talk with this man, and he stated that he had told the manager and his friend that the work had to be done as he was doing it.

The first thing I asked our managing engineer was to ask our land engineer if the land engineer he had brought knew that he had to work in compliance with our procedures and strategies. And he answered affirmatively. So I asked them if they had been there making sure that he was carrying out the job following the procedures. And they answered that they had understood that that man worked on his own and that there was no need to observe his work. Then I asked: what had happened if you had checked his work from the beginning? They answered that what really happened wouldn´t have happened.

I told them to go right away to talk to this person and to ask him to carry out his job according to the strategy previously established for the task. They answered that they had already talked to him and that he had stubbornly answered that that was the way he was used to doing things and that there was no other possible alternative.

It was then that I asked via telephone to gather all the main leaders of the organization, especially this man. I wanted to have the meeting behind closed doors in the morning of the following day.

The first thing I mentioned was that what they had done was not only their problem because I also felt responsible for this lack of supervision in the execution of procedures and strategies. It was then when this man with a huge ego, told me that what they were doing was correct. I answered that if it was ok we wouldn´t be talking to revert the situation. Then I asked if they would change the real strategy and they answered positively. Then I asked if the delay we had at that moment could be compensated and with how many additional people. They answered and so we did.

Which is the lesson learnt after all this journey? The lesson is that if we had made sure from the beginning, supervising, measuring advances, checking the strategy, we wouldn´t have had the problems we in fact had.

Finally, after 2 days everything was going back to normal. However, more workers had to be included to stabilize the situation. In spite of this, to be able to complete the job around the agreed date, we had to work at full throttle. Attitude works miracles, that´s why I want to state in writing 2 rules that will always help entrepreneurs.

1. The first rule we can learn from this anecdote is that there is always a better plan. We always need good planning. There are many ways to achieve satisfactory results, so don´t let people ignore your plans. Everything has to be aligned with a good attitude, conviction and determination.
2. The second is that we shouldn´t be flexible if we already have a plan and a strategy. If this managing engineer had supervised from the first day the strategy this wouldn´t have happened and we would have finished in due time and form.

It is fundamental to work on communications with collaborators before carrying out any activity.

Look upwards

Bear in mind that the entrepreneur´s growth is not achieved from his office only.

What does looking upwards mean for an entrepreneur?

There are two ways of looking at the acts of an entrepreneur, looking inwards or downwards and looking outwards or upwards.

The first one is the vision of the company´s course of action, the vision of employees, of finance and sales, of acts and of "our" clients and suppliers. It is the description of our course of action.

The second one is the vision of where the company acts the vision of the industry, the geographical location where it operates and of competitors.

The first one is useful to assess how efficient we are, the second one allows us to determine what we have to do to be competitive and gain markets.

The 95% of entrepreneurs only has an inwards vision, and so they ignore which percentage of the market they have and if they are losing participation in the industry and the country. Only the 5% of businessmen understand the global vision: the downwards vision plus the upwards vision.

In economic terms, this means to have a macroeconomic vision that comprises industries, internal gross product and inflation versus the microeconomic vision which only takes into consideration the analysis of our company's particular features.

Momentum

We always have to pay attention to the opportunities that may arise.

We have to be constantly going over the opportunities that appear in life. There is no way of missing the opportunity to make changes if we are paying attention to the favorable situations that may arise in life. This is called Momentum or timely moment.

Successful people say that this moment comes for two reasons:

One is due to the ability to be at the right time.

The other is due to the search and pursuit of possibilities in a constant way. Like this the moment we really want to come in life will arrive.

If you work steadily, with intelligence, perseverance and determination you will be able to attract his moment.

I suggest you look for it and remember that the moment you have always expected will definitely get to your life.

Negotiation

Always look for a way to unify people´s criteria to be able to come up with your best product or service.
When you want to take a big step in life, first think carefully which the greatest obstacles might be, and analyze as well which may be the major benefits.

If you want to be a brilliant businessman you should first negotiate with life what you want to be. This will be the starting point to close any deal, negotiation, commercial situation or anything you want to negotiate.

The best negotiation is the one in which all the parties win. You can do it; you just have to think how you would like to be treated if you were on the other side of the negotiation. This is called a "Win-Win". A win-win negotiation implies fair and beneficial terms for all the parties involved, without trying to get any kind of advantage or benefit from the other.

Once the negotiation is settled, it is fundamental to provide the best service you can offer and the best assistance. You have to be outstanding in your job and you have to achieve empathy.

To be able to close important deals you should carry out negotiations in a good way.

Sometimes we concentrate on closing deals quickly without thinking in what our client really needs today or might need in the future; we do not concentrate on living the door open and paving the way for future deals.

It is fundamental to take into account that some time you might be at the other side of the table and you will want to be offered the best service.

Negotiating is not difficult; we have to be fair and give the best of us. There is a popular phrase that summarizes perfectly well the bases of good negotiations: treat the others in the same way you want to be treated.

Complex Situations

When you go through complex situations outside your company, remember that you will always have additional drawbacks that will try to defeat you. You have to find the way to apply the same faith and perseverance you have resorted to your previous businesses.
Simple as it seems, it is really complicated. For each problem in life the first thing to do is to summon a meeting to analyze the situation.

It is fundamental to have meetings because you can get useful information of which you can take advantage to prepare a cost analysis, a sales projection, a cost reduction, an investment plan, a meeting to analyze your company´s situation, a meeting to praise a member of your company, etc.

My advice is to call meetings on a permanent basis, wherever you are and whatever you are doing, any kind of meeting, even with your beloved ones. Think of the benefits this brings about.

Sometimes we need to travel thousands of kilometers to talk to a client for different reasons, we often need to do it, for the sake of the commitment we have.

If there is something we learn in life is that the past is already past. The important thing is to try to understand and see what can be done **today** looking at **tomorrow.**

Long and monotonous courtesy talks have to be avoided not to waste our time and the time of the others.

We have to keep in mind that life is beautiful and, that if for any reason we have stressful meetings, we have to avoid them simply by changing the language and giving explanations and emphasizing that everything can be discussed to reach agreements by using simple words but with a profound intensity.

Get out of a business

In the same way in which it is necessary to know how to start a new business, in my case create it, it is also necessary to know when it is the proper time to get out of it.

It is very common to see people doing business completely ignoring how to get out of them. And I think ... it is the same as starting to study something without knowing how many subjects or years it will take to graduate, it is like cooking without knowing the number of people who will eat or like buying paint without knowing how many walls need to be painted. Going out of a business means to understand who might be interested in our company if we have to sell it, when it is the best moment to do it and under which circumstances.

I will mention the story of a friend who had important fluctuations in his companies and always said: "Businesses are not our children". He meant that we take care of children in good and bad times, in health and in illness and forever. But this does not apply to business. It is important to know when a business will not make any profits and be prepared to get rid of it. If not, we will become compulsive bettors always thinking that in the next move we can recover what has been invested. One thing is to work in order to make a profit and a different one is to work to recover what has been invested ... and unfortunately when a business does not make profits we end up investing amounts that will never be recovered.

It is also important to know that your partners at present will not necessarily be your partners in the future. We can sell part of a company but it is important to know that with a good contract it can be acquired again. We can change partners as the business grows or changes and this is very positive.

Sometimes, when your business is well positioned in the market, you can sell only your company´s brand and leave the assets out of the negotiation.

If you are to have a partner, make sure he shares your philosophy and understands the real needs of the clients. If you are considering expansion, I hope your partner shares the same view. You might have not taken this detail into account and, your partner may not want to do it, in which case, you´d better imagine this scenario beforehand.

It is clear that many people do not want to expand because they are afraid of uncertainty, so we have to develop a way of satisfying this need and the answer is by making contributions to the industry that will add value. There are partners who are very good at being the owners of a single company and some others would like to replicate them.

To get out of business, it is necessary to be flexible and open minded. It is difficult to think that we know everything we have to know when we start our journey. It is even harder to imagine when we start our journey where it will end.

The important thing is to know how to move forward. It is not important to know what we can´t even imagine. Technology is an example of this. It is impossible to know when a new invention that will change industry or make it obsolete will appear; but we have to be always flexible, open minded and updated.

Value

You always have to be at the service of people. This will give you more confidence in your acts.

A businessman works in a village and in a country, with the idea of exporting one day to help this village and country grow. To make his dream come true he has to identify the values of the government officials that get on well with the business world.

- Support the long term. Officials change, but businessmen are committed in the long term. A businessman cannot resign and stop paying salaries because he is not doing well. You always have to solve issues and the appropriate way of thinking is in the long term.
- Stop waiting for the government to offer you money, while you pay for taxes, inflation or interest rates. Help start a new business, **export**. Growing means expanding, not working longer hours.
- Facilitate scenarios for growing. It is not understandable to do everything at the same time with the same taxes.
- Optimize the number of hours you spend commuting and the number of hours that are wasted when trying to do everything

from 9 to 18: banks, working, school, and health issues.
- Educate about what debt is. If a family consisting of a father, a mother and 2 children were in debt, what would be the purpose of the parents´ arguing and asking each other for money? What would be the point of both parents asking their children for help and the children asking their parents for help? Wouldn´t it be high time the parents went out and brought some money and the children looked after the house? Please, encourage officials to create the conditions to go "out".
- Pay tribute to the Pareto Principle, the famous rule of 80-20. Do something with the 80% of your time; go on doing what you have been doing so far and with the remaining 20% work on growing.
- Enjoy Mondays, which represent the beginning of a new week. Ask workers to recommend actions for the week that might teach others. Teaching is the most powerful action to learn.
- Think of patents. At least of one collective patent on behalf of the company representing your country. At least one per year and in which everybody can participate. THIS APPEARS TO BE SIMPLE BUT COULD BE THE STARTING POINT TO MAKE A COUNTRY GROW IN VARIOUS

GENERATIONS. Patents last for 20 years and licensing them generates income.
- Starting new businesses means to know how to invest. It means knowing that we have to make an investment at the beginning of a project, either in training, materials, property, patents or methodologies and that this investment will be amortized in the medium and long term or when the company is sold.
- Example: I buy a property to set up a business at the top floor. This investment is different from the original business. They are 2 businesses in one, the value of the property (which we wish will increase over the years) and the value of the business (we try it to cover fix cost first and then to yield some produce).
- What value should the investment give? It must allow us to be different, to create a differential value.
- Cash flow is essential to manage a company. There is only one thing we need to know, that no matter how small our company may be, we must have a projection of expenditure and income.

Variety

Do not forget that to be better in what you do you should try hard to find new ways of doing things.

Markets are dynamic. This means that their needs change constantly. A company that wishes to last in time must not only be able to adjust to these changes but also to anticipate to them.

Offering a wide variety of services is fundamental for a company, but not any service. A good businessman develops new products listening to his clients, understanding his problems, needs, and desires and based on them, creating services to offer solutions and help them grow.

For those interested in going deeper into this subject, I recommend the rule of the three verbs: LISTEN, INVESTIGATE, and ANSWER.

Why do I mention the 3 verbs? Because it is fundamental to answer only after some research has been done before. Many people DON´T LISTEN and only ANSWER. Why don´t we go deeper into the subject before answering?

Vision

If you have a small business in mind, this will certainly become a reality. However, if the vision of your dreams and objectives is broader, more doors will open for you.

In business terminology, vision refers to the goals and objectives a company has and expects to achieve in the future. It consists of an ideal expectation that reflects the plan of what is wanted for the future.

Vision reflects what is expected of the future of the company and sets some guidelines to follow to achieve the desired results.

The one who defines the vision of a company is the businessman, partner or shareholder in a company. Clearly, they are who establish the future vision. Now, those who support this vision are all the leaders, collaborators and especially the marketing team.

It is vital that your vision is always as broad as possible, for only like this will you have big and intense dreams.

Don´t let anybody make negative remarks about your vision, because everybody will have to make efforts to get to the end of the road.

Skills

All of us have different skills. Sometimes we are unaware of them but, when we are in an uncomfortable situation we discover our great skills.

SUGGESTIONS FOR ENTREPRENEURS

Constant Improvement

Do not feel completely satisfied with your studies. Try to improve your skills.

Every change takes time and a change of culture. This change of culture must be undergone implementing a program that has to be sustained for many years. If you seek to create a culture of continuous improvement for your company, you need passion, patience and planning. These are my suggestions:

- **Dream.**
- **Take the future into account.**
- **Write your mission.**
- **Gather courage, positive thinking and a good attitude.**
- **Think about your past.**
- **Communicate a global vision.**
- **Provide clear instructions.**
- **Transform your mission into your business and personal mantra.**
- **Start with small improvements instead of big changes at a big scale.**
- **Be constant.**
- **Be your vision and teach it with your example.**
- **Generate wish.**
- **Allow experimentation**
- **Encourage the professional and personal objectives of your coworkers.**

- Demonstrate you appreciate your employees, suppliers and clients in public.

Marketing

Every time you elaborate a product or service, remember that it is ideal to show it to the market. However nowadays what most draws people´s attention in advertising is to be simple but with deep contents. And also bear in mind that you can´t extend Marketing too much.

Creation of a brand

When you are starting a company you have to become your brand, people will recognize you.

Branding or the creation of a brand is related to the perception the client has when he hears or thinks about our company, more specifically about its name. Its name is the brand. The word brand can be defined as something alive that evolves and with which quality and the level of satisfaction can be measured taking into consideration the behavior of clients and their ecosystem.

The brand of a company must fulfill the following objectives:

- Delivering the message clearly
- Reinforcing its credibility
- Connecting emotionally the company with real and potential clients
- Encouraging the client to continue recommending and using it
- Building clients´ loyalty

To develop a brand successfully, the needs and desires of the clients must be understood. The creation of a brand takes place when its message is integrated with all the points of public contact. Brands do not only create loyal clients and loyal employees and partners; they also create loyal suppliers and communities. Brands communicate a mission in which to believe, something to support. They help understand the purpose of the company.

Personality

Remember that you will always need marketing for your products or services. The first thing you have to take into account is that your personality must be represented.

We all have a defined personality. In my case, I always encourage people to feel the need to grow and gather positive images.

As this is my personality, I am composed of a set of ways of being, which together with my dreams constitute my possible being.

I also want my companies to have my personality and so I want my collaborators to be the image of the company.

By printing my personality into my companies, they do not only fulfill projects but grow with enthusiasm, stand up again when they fall and organize the clients´ tasks as I have always done since I started as an apprentice. I consider my companies the clients´ helpers, trying to be better and looking after their appearance. I think of my companies and I remember what my mother used to tell me: that I should always have some money and nice looks, as I could be judged by my appearance.

Companies might also be judged by what they represent for people, suppliers, clients, everybody. It is necessary to act and transmit trust; this will be of great help when they want to evaluate you as a company.

Real time

For the sake of good marketing and to increase your clients you have to do the right thing every day.

It is useless to plan beforehand if we lose the ability to work on our image every day.

I have learnt that, when we work continuously, second after second, this is called *real time*.

Marketing is the group of actions we do to promote our services and increase our invoicing. So, why doing it only when we need it or when we are motivated? We should do it always, at every moment.

It is essential that our collaborators understand that they need constant marketing with our clients. However, it is even more important to be coherent and truthful with words and actions. Do we by any chance know when it is a right moment? The right moment is always, every day, in real time.

Somewhere else in this book I talked about the importance of the heart. The heart beats thousands of times in an hour. The heart works in real time, it does not rest. Marketing has to be like this, as the heart, in real time.

Innovation

Thinking creatively will help you find new opportunities.

Many times I had the opportunity to talk with my leaders and managers and I have always transmitted a message I hope may also be useful for.

Sometimes coworkers tell me they have many problems with the contracts. When this happens I tell them that even if they have problems, a problem might be an opportunity.

I always mention that it is very important to do a simple exercise which helps a lot and consists in writing down all the problems you have and looking for at least three possible solutions for each problem. Once we have the three main solutions; this will help us find definitively the solutions to the problems.

For a very long time I have been talking to the people in my organization and telling them that they have to work as a team to make things work. And, which is the main reason to make this group exercise? The reason is that it can be applied to absolutely every issue. If you implement this dynamics you will be able to search solutions to all our processes. This means that, for each situation that needs to be improved you will have to look for three alternatives.

Suppose a team comprises 9 people. If they introduce a situation to be improved and look for three solutions each, at the end of the exercise the team will have 27 possible alternatives to be able to find the solution.

I frequently hear clients ask us to be creative and to innovate. Likewise, I also prepare my collaborators to look for alternatives of innovation in our internal processes to help our clients improve. Obviously, the same exercise can be done with the client, looking for his greatest problems and showing him that we have different alternatives to solve them. This will undoubtedly help our client feel supported by the commitment we demonstrated.

I also need to mention that these exercises help make our minds quicker and find alternate roads which can make things simpler in any realm of our lives no matter how complex they appear to be.

Without pressure

You should always empower your coworkers so that they feel important and could reverse results without pressing.

Results are the assessment of the objectives we have set.

There is no good management if in the end, results don´t prove to be the expected ones. I want to eradicate the negative image of results. I would like to find the positive value of results. Even when I have lost a lot of time and money due to projects drawbacks, a look on them without any pressure allows me to stand on my feet again and grow. If I have had a bad management, I want it to set the basis for a good one. Without adverse results, I wouldn´t have grown.

I ask you then, whenever you want to implement something in your company, to make sure your collaborators listen to you and pay attention. With this devoted attention they can carry out what you are asking for, because otherwise you won´t be able to improve your performance and you will keep on obtaining the same results. This certainly means that we all need to get involved.

One more dream

Educate

I am going to create an Academy where thousands of people can get training.

This initiative is coming to life right now, after noticing that good specialists are getting old and have not, who knows why, continued to contribute with their experience to the world of industry where our main services are focused on satisfying our clients´ needs.

Besides, even if this industry is always in demand of specialized and qualified people, courses do not offer all the knowledge required for a technical job. They deal with and comprise only theoretical knowledge and this does not guarantee success in spite of long years of study.

I have already said that my life circumstances did not allow me to have a university education. The poverty and loneliness of my mother as a single adult in charge of several children and my deep love, respect and adoration for her made me choose to work and help at home and this was undoubtedly a unique decision. Nevertheless, I did get a lot of training. I learnt, as it is said, "making my own path, as I moved on". I trained at different jobs learning from the others, from their success and failure, listening and looking attentively. Later on, when I had the means, I did have access to varied formal training.

I know, from my own experience, how hard it is to be the helper of specialists. But learning from them is like attending a field Academy and forging oneself in ardent fire. Graduating in this field academy represented a real university of life.

So, I felt I had to take training to the workplace and encourage my most valued workers to teach apart from working. It is there where we learn the most, where we can learn from those who are working in big projects.

Due to this, my academy has the objective of combining job training and practice at the same place and, the best place I can imagine for this is my company. My dream is to create a Company-Academy and, I want through my example to inspire other companies to develop the talent of people and give working opportunities to their graduates.

My personal objective is by teaching and helping, to inspire those with my same vision not only to bring out the best version of them but also to bring out the best version of the others.

Formal education in general, does not reflect the needs of know-how and real solutions of companies, for what is acquired in concrete projects cannot be fully acquired in academies. They do not offer all the information and practice required.

This evidences the need of a better relation between academic training and practical know-how, which will facilitate the introduction of specialists in the business world.

My dream is to take advantage of the learning opportunities present at my company, which has the solutions to the real problems of the industry. For this reason, my new project is the creation of a Company-Academy, by means of which my company can be at the same time an academy. It will be the place where learning relates more directly to "demand", focusing on the one hand on empiric practices and on the other on permanent updating, which is vital in times of technological changes, globalization and markets with a high demand of complex jobs.

My objective is the articulation between a successful company with projects under execution and practicing professionals that work as a professional training unit.

This collaboration is highly useful. According to María Antonia Gallart and as stated in her article "School-Company: a difficult and yet necessary relationship" article published in the Bulletin of Education and Work, Latin American Network of Education and Work CIID - CENEP Year 7 - N°1 - Buenos Aires - June 1996, it says:

> *"The reasons for the convenience of Companies-Schools lie in the potentialities and limitations each of these organizations —educational institutions and productive organizations- have for people´s training*

processes. Schools and, in general every institution organized to develop a training program through a lengthy period of time, tend to have an organizational permanence that acquires pseudo-bureaucratic forms; their division of work takes special characteristics from the pedagogic relationship teacher-student; their curricular structure has a strong academic-disciplinary trait; vertical linking –in the case of formal education- makes superior levels influence the objectives of intermediate levels, even if for some students these are terminal. All these characteristics favor the exclusion of significant content in middle education in countries strongly oriented towards university studies."

Instead, a company is by definition the arena of productive tasks and, it is for this reason that the company better knows what is needed to carry out jobs with excellence.

A company should invest its personnel´s time in comprehensive training. On the one hand, it should offer theoretical knowledge for intellectual competences and practical knowledge required to be successful at work and on the other, practice at real scenarios.

My Company-Academy plans to implement a teaching-learning process through the company, where I will offer all my knowledge, my strongest will, my positive thinking and my conviction to create a place that will facilitate the acquisition of general competences and specific competences, both of which are necessary, today more than ever, due to the polyvalence and flexibility of the working market.

To feel that my mission as a businessman is complete, I think I need to contribute to the learning process in my industry. In my personal case, it was my mother who shared numerous lessons with me, which later on helped me grow. The lessons of my mother gave me a good heart and plenty of courage. But being the helper of a specialist in my job was fundamental since it taught me all the necessary skills.

Patricio Rozas

Studies

- Basic and Middle School.
- My first job as a qualified welder in all welding processes.
- I attended courses on accounting, tax, human resources and business management.

Business Skills.

- Elaboration of budgets in a 10-minute conversation involving millions of dollars.
- Planning of a project from its onset to its termination on a board and explaining it up to its completion.
- Problem solving with great number of participants involved.
- Assistance to engineers to overcome drawbacks in projects performance.

Specialization Courses

- Basic and Advanced Accounting.
- Tax – Management Level.
- Human Resources
- High Performance Reading and advanced course on Fast Reading and Photo Reading.
- Lecturing and Public Speaking, Conventional Method and NLP Method.
- Training Unleash the Power within (2018 and 2019), Business Mastery (2019), Date with Destiny (2019) with Tony Robbins.
- Trainer of Neuro-linguistic Programming coaches. (NLP) with JOHN GRINDER.

www.ingramcontent.com/pod-product-compliance
Lightning Source LLC
Chambersburg PA
CBHW070618220526
45466CB00001B/48